# Campus English 102

# Campus English 102

Charles Kim
Jieun Hwang
Yoondo Bae

SHINGU PUBLISHING CO.

## Preface

Welcome to Campus English 102, the second installment in our series of textbooks tailored for university students in Korea. Building upon the foundation laid in Campus English 101, this book continues to focus on honing your English language skills through engaging lessons relevant to student life and real-world situations.

Similar to its predecessor, Campus English 102 is structured into 12 units, each designed to be completed in a two-hour class or extended with supplementary material for longer periods. This textbook maintains a consistent structure, allowing both students and teachers to anticipate the sequence of sections and objectives from unit to unit.

## Unit Structure:

1. **Warm-up:** Kick off each unit with an interactive warm-up activity to spark your interest and set the tone for the lesson ahead.

2. **Vocabulary:** Expand your vocabulary with topic-oriented words crucial for effective communication in various contexts.

3. **Grammar Focus:** Delve into key grammar points essential for expressing yourself accurately and fluently in English.

**4. Pattern Practice:** Apply the grammar concepts learned through speaking and writing exercises tailored to reinforce your understanding.

**5. Dialogue (Listening and Speaking):** Sharpen your listening and speaking skills by engaging with authentic dialogues that mirror real-life scenarios.

**6. Reading:** Enhance your reading comprehension abilities with texts relevant to university life, accompanied by audio support for pronunciation practice.

**7. Conversation Practice:** Strengthen your conversational skills through interactive speaking activities centered on unit themes.

**8. Editing:** Test your mastery of language targets through exercises designed to identify and correct errors, fostering a deeper understanding of grammar and syntax.

**Review Units:** Units 6 and 12 provide comprehensive reviews of previously learned material to prepare you for assessments and gauge your progress.

**Workbook:** Supplement your learning with the accompanying workbook, offering additional exercises and practice opportunities to reinforce concepts covered in each unit.

Whether you're a beginner or continuing your English language journey, Campus English 102 is here to support your growth and development. We hope you find this textbook enriching and enjoyable as you embark on this language-learning adventure.

# Table of Contents

Unit 01

# Who is your uncle?

**Warm-up:** How many members are in your family? Share your family members with your partner.

### My Family Tree

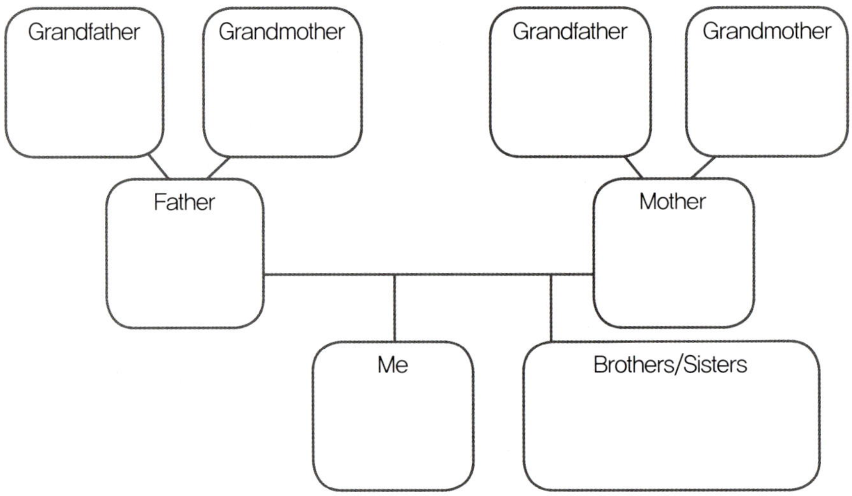


## Vocabulary 1:

| | | | | |
|---|---|---|---|---|
| mother | father | grandfather | grandmother | brother |
| sister | son | daughter | aunt | uncle |
| cousin | niece | nephew | husband | wife |
| in-law | relative | only child | children | |

## Grammar Focus 1: Possessive Form (소유격)



| We use the possessive form ('s) to show ownership. | |
|---|---|
| Mary's pencil case<br>Ron's guitar<br>Chris' game | the dog's toy<br>the boy's parents<br>the parents' cars |

## Pattern Practice 1a:

Find Terry and then complete the sentences below.

1. Erin is Terry's ______________ niece ______________.
2. Lou is Terry's ____________________________.
3. Rod is Terry's ____________________________.
4. Oliver is Terry's ____________________________.
5. Roger is Terry's ____________________________.
6. Rebecca is Terry's ____________________________.
7. Charles is Terry's ____________________________.
8. Bonnie is Terry's ____________________________.
9. Eddie is Terry's ____________________________.
10. Helen is Terry's ____________________________.

## Pattern Practice 1b:

Find Terry's relatives and then label what their relationship is to him.

1. Sally ______ *cousin*
2. Shirly ______ ______
3. Warren ______ ______
4. Kim ______ ______
5. Julie ______ ______

## Grammar Focus 2: Possessive Form (소유격) and Possessive Pronouns (소유 대명사)

We use possessive form and possessive pronouns to show ownership **(소유권)**.

| Pronoun | Possessive Form | Example | Possessive Pronoun | Example |
|---|---|---|---|---|
| I | my | That's my car. | mine | It's mine. |
| We | our | That's our house. | ours | It's ours. |
| You | your | That's your job. | yours | It's yours. |
| He | his | That's his wallet. | his | It's his. |
| She | her | That's her mirror. | hers | It's hers. |
| They | their | That's their school. | theirs | It's theirs. |
| It | its | Jeju Island (it) is famous for its oranges. | | |

**Note:** The possessive pronoun "theirs" cannot be used with people.
The teacher is theirs.
This sentence is incorrect because "theirs" cannot show possession of people.

## Pattern Practice 2:

Practice the following patterns. Use the hints and then try to practice without the hints.



**1.** *aunt, Irene*

a. Who's that?

b. That's my aunt.

c. What's her name?

d. Her name is Irene.

**2.** *brother, Jessie*

a. Who's that?

b. That's ________ ________.

c. What's ________ name?

d. ________ name is Jessie.

**3.** *sister-in-law, Robin*

a. Who's that?

b. ________ ________ ________.

c. What's ________ ________?

d. ________ ________ is ________.

**4.** *nephew, Eric*

a. ________ ________?

b. ________ ________ ________.

c. ________ ________ ________?

d. ________ ________ ________ ________.

**5.** *son, John*

a. ________ ________?

b. ________ ________ ________.

c. ________ ________ ________?

d. ________ ________ ________ ________.

## Pattern Practice 3:

Practice the following patterns. Use the hints and then try to practice without the hints.

**1.** *bicycle, I, sister*

a. Who owns that bicycle?

b. That's my sister's bicycle. It's hers.

c. Oh really? I didn't know that was your sister's bicycle.

**2.** *jacket, Jenny, brother*

a. Who owns that ____________?

b. That's Jenny's ____________ jacket. It's ______.

c. Oh really? I didn't know that was ____________ ______ __________.

**3.** *juice, I, cousin*

a. Who owns that ______________?

b. That's __________ ______________ ______________. It's _____________.

c. Oh really? ____ _______ _______ ______ _____ ______ _______ _____.

**4.** *house, Dale, parents*

a. ______________________________________?

b. ______________________________________. _____________.

c. ______________? ______________________________________.

**5.** *dog, I, niece*

a. ______________________________________?

b. ______________________________________. _____________.

c. ______________? ______________________________________.

## Dialogue (Listening and Speaking):

Listen to the dialogue and fill in the missing words. Then practice the dialogue with your partner twice.

| |
|---|
| **Diane:** Hi Shirley! Who is that girl over there? |
| **Shirley:** Oh, she's my sister's daughter. |
| **Diane:** Is she your (1) ______________________? |
| **Shirley:** Yes, she's my **niece**. And that boy next to her is my sister's son. |
| **Diane:** So, Is he your (2) _______________________? |
| **Shirley:** Yes, he's my **nephew**. The dog they're playing with is (3) _________________. |
| **Diane:** Your family is big! |
| **Shirley:** Yes, it is! What about (4) _____________________________? |
| **Diane:** Mine? I guess (5) ________________ family is big too. |

**Key Words:** niece 조카(여) / nephew 조카(남)

## Reading: Read the following story and then answer the questions.

### A Family Visit

My wife Jane **invited** her mom to stay with us for the summer. Her dad, brother, sister-in-law, and cousins are coming too. My son and daughter will share their rooms, but they're **excited**.

"Clean up your toys and put them away." I told my daughter. "But these aren't mine." she said. "They're his." She pointed to her brother. "Yes." he said. "These toys aren't hers. They're mine."

There was a Barbie doll on the floor. "Is that yours?" I asked him. "Well, no." he said. "That's not my Barbie doll. It's hers, but I **borrowed** it." My son felt **embarrassed**. He picked up the Barbie doll and gave it back to his sister.

"Thanks." she said. "This is mine. I'll put it in my room."

"Okay." I said. "Let's clean up the house. Your grandmother, grandfather, uncle, and aunt will be here soon. We want our house to be clean. This house is ours, and we want them to see our clean house."

**Key Words:** invited 초대했다 / excited 흥분한 / borrowed 빌렸다 / embarrassed 당황한

## Reading Questions:

**1.** Who did Jane invite to stay for the summer?

Jane invited her ______________________________.

**2.** Whose toys were on the floor?

The ______________ toys were on the floor.

3. What did the son borrow from his sister?

   He borrowed his sister's ______________________________.

4. How did the son feel?

   He felt ______________________________.

5. What did the daughter do with the Barbie doll?

   She put it in ______________________________.

## Conversation Practice: Ask and answer the questions with a partner.

1. How many members are in your family?
2. Do you have any brothers or sisters?
3. How many cousins do you have?
4. Do you have any nephews or nieces?
5. Are you an only child?

## Editing: Find and correct the errors in the following sentences.

1. Stacy picked up hers doll and put it in hers sister hands.

2. I bought a new laptop. This laptop is my.

3. The Koreans flew theirs country's flag on Independence Day.

4. Mine cousin is coming to mine house to visit.

5. What's yours phone number? Can I save it in mine phone?

Unit **02**

# Is there a coffee shop?

## Warm up:

Find six different things in each picture.

***Example:*** There is a purple rose.

## Vocabulary 1a:

Match the words with the pictures.

a. coffee shop　　b. cafeteria　　c. art gallery
d. amusement park　　e. bookstore　　f. office　　g. gym
h. convenience store　　i. locker　　j. department office(학과 사무실)

1. 

______________________

2. 

______________________

3. 

______________________

4. 

______________________

5. 

______________________

6. 

______________________

7. 

______________________

8. 

______________________

9. 

______________________

10. 

______________________

## Vocabulary 1b:

Match the places with the things you can do there.

1. a coffee shop: ________
2. a cafeteria: ________
3. an art gallery: ________
4. an amusement park: ________
5. a bookstore: ________
6. an office: ________
7. a gym: ________
8. a convenience store: ________
9. a department office: ________
10. a locker: ________

a. enjoy lunch with classmates
b. work on assignments and projects
c. ride roller coaster and play games
d. exercise and lift weights
e. drink coffee and study with friends
f. look and buy books and magazines
g. buy snacks and drinks
h. enjoy paintings
i. students can keep their books here
j. students can get help or information

## Grammar Focus 1:

We use ***there is*** and ***there are*** to show if something is present or if it's here.

| Singular (단수) | Plural (복수) |
|---|---|
| There is a book on the table.<br>There isn't a cat in the kitchen. | There are books on the table.<br>There aren't any cats in the kitchen. |

## Pattern Practice 1:

Fill in the blanks using ***There is*** or ***There are***.

1. ________________________ a bookstore on campus.
2. ________________________ two cafeterias on campus.
3. ________________________ a gym next to the cafeteria.
4. ________________________ many convenience stores.
5. ________________________ the professor's office.

## Grammar Focus 2:

***There was*** and ***there were*** are the past forms of ***there is*** and ***there are***. We use them to form sentences about the existence or presence of something in the past.

| Singular (단수) | Plural (복수) |
|---|---|
| There was a pen on the table.<br>There was a good movie on TV. | There were pens on the table.<br>There were fireworks at the park last night. |

## Pattern Practice 2:

Fill in the blanks using ***There was*** or ***There were***.

1. ________________ a nice restaurant in the city last night.
2. ________________ many people at the art gallery last weekend.
3. ________________ nice coffee shops when we traveled in Australia.
4. ________________ a good convenience store, but now it's gone.
5. ________________ many luxury hotels, but now they're old.

## Grammar Focus 3:

We use ***is there*** and ***are there*** to form questions about the existence or presence of something.

| Singular (단수) | Plural (복수) |
|---|---|
| Is there a pen on the table?<br>Was there a pen on the table? | Are there pens on the table?<br>Were there pens on the table? |

## Pattern Practice 3:

Fill in the blanks using ***is there***, ***are there***, ***was there***, or ***were there***.

1. ____________________ any convenience stores near your house?
2. ____________________ an amusement park when you traveled last week?
3. ____________________ coffee shops near school?
4. ____________________ any students at school last weekend?
5. ____________________ a hospital near school?

## Pattern Practice 4:

Write affirmative sentences using ***there is*** and ***there are***. Also, write negative sentences using ***there isn't*** and ***there aren't***.

*Ex.*

*There is a computer on the desk.*

*There isn't a printer on the desk.*

1.

There is ____________________

There isn't ____________________

2.

______________________

______________________

3.

______________________

______________________

## Dialogue (Listening and Speaking):

Listen to the dialogue and fill in the missing words. Then practice the dialogue with your partner twice.

| | |
|---|---|
| Frank: | Hey Nicole, did you go to the beach and see the **sunset**? |
| Nicole: | No, I didn't. What was it like? |
| Frank: | It was great! (1) ______________ so many beautiful colors in the sky. |
| Nicole: | Really? Like what? |
| Frank: | Well, during sunset, (2) ____________________colors of orange, pink, and purple in the sky. |
| Nicole: | Wow, that sounds amazing! (3) __________________ many people there? |
| Frank: | Yes, (4) ______________________ many! People came to watch the sunset and took photos. |
| Nicole: | I love taking photos of **nature**. I want to go to a beach sunset someday. |
| Frank: | Yes! (5) ______________________ **peace** and quiet. |
| Nicole: | Sounds like a perfect way to relax. |
| Frank: | Exactly! It's a special moment every time you watch the sunset at the beach. |

**Key Words:** sunset 일몰 / nature 자연 / peace 평화

## **Reading:** Read the following story and then answer the questions.

### A Busy Place

Changi Airport is a big and busy airport in Singapore. There are many things to see and do at Changi Airport.

Inside the terminal, there are many shops and restaurants. There is also a lot of space for people to walk around. People from all over the world come to Changi Airport.

If you are hungry, there are **plenty** of food choices. There are fast food restaurants, cafes, and **fancy** restaurants. There are also shops and you can buy **souvenirs** and gifts there.

There are many things to do **while** you wait for your flight. There are gardens with beautiful flowers and plants. There are also places where you can relax and **take a nap**.

Changi Airport is a special place. There is always something happening and something new to **discover**. It is a busy and exciting place to visit!

**Key Words:** plenty 충분한 / fancy 고급스러운 / souvenirs 기념품 / while ~하는 동안 / take a nap 낮잠을 자다 / discover 발견하다

## Reading Questions:

**1.** Where is Changi Airport?

______________________________

**2.** What is inside the terminal?

______________________________

3. What food choices are there?

______________________________________________

4. Are there any shops to buy souvenirs?

______________________________________________

5. Are there any things to do while you wait for your flight?

______________________________________________

**Conversation Practice:** Work together with a partner and find five differences.

**Editing:** Find and correct the errors in the following sentences.

1. There are a pen on the table.

2. There is many restaurants near school.

3. Are their any baseball teams in Korea?

4. They're students eating in the cafeteria.

5. There isn't many taxis in the morning.

Unit 03

# What's he like?

**Warm-up:** People come in all different shapes, sizes and personalities. With a partner, take turns describing each picture. Use the words below.

1. 

2. 

3. 

## Vocabulary 1:

Match the words in the chart with their explanations on page 25.

| Appearance (외모) | Character (성격) |
|---|---|
| 1. ___ muscular | 1. ___ shy |
| 2. ___ petite | 2. ___ friendly |
| 3. ___ slim | 3. ___ smart |
| 4. ___ chubby | 4. ___ lazy |
| 5. ___ tall | 5. ___ funny |
| 6. ___ short | 6. ___ serious |
| 7. ___ handsome | 7. ___ diligent |
| 8. ___ pretty | 8. ___ stubborn |
| 9. ___ elderly | 9. ___ patient |
| 10. ___ young | 10. ___ reliable |

Explanations of the words in the chart on page 24.

a. hard working

b. 185cm

c. afraid to talk to people

d. ha ha ha ha

e. 70 years old

f. never laughs

g. well-developed muscles

h. good looking man

i. it's okay to wait

j. good looking woman

k. 10 years old

l. a little fat

m. doesn't want to change

n. 130cm

o. small and slim in size

p. hates to work

q. not too fat, not too skinny

r. enjoys other people

s. quick thinker

t. always there when needed

**Word bank:**

Can you think of more words that describe people?

| Appearance (외모) | Character (성격) |
|---|---|
| 1. ______ | 6. ______ |
| 2. ______ | 7. ______ |
| 3. ______ | 8. ______ |
| 4. ______ | 9. ______ |
| 5. ______ | 10. ______ |

## Vocabulary 2 (Hair and facial features)

| hair shape and styling (머리 모양과 스타일링) | hair color (머리 색) | facial features (얼굴 특징) |
|---|---|---|
| straight hair<br>wavy hair<br>curly hair<br>pony tail<br>bald | blonde<br>brunette | freckles<br>eyelashes<br>eyebrows<br>mustache<br>beard |

Fill in the blanks with the correct word.

**1.** 말총머리: ____________________ **7.** 속눈썹: ____________________

**2.** 눈썹: ____________________ **8.** 직모머리: ____________________

**3.** 대머리: ____________________ **9.** 주근깨: ____________________

**4.** 갈색머리: ____________________ **10.** 금발: ____________________

**5.** 콧수염: ____________________ **11.** 수염: ____________________

**6.** 곱슬머리: ____________________ **12.** 웨이브머리: ____________________

## Grammar Focus 1: Adjectives (형용사)

An **adjective** is a word that modifies or describes a noun. It usually comes **before** the noun it modifies. It can be a word, a phrase, or a clause. Adjectives answer these **five questions**:

**Which one?** ***Example:*** I bought ***that*** coat.

**Note:** Only four adjectives answer this question: *this, that, these, and those.*

**What kind (of)?** ***Example:*** He likes ***oatmeal*** cookies.

**How many?** ***Example:*** ***Two*** boys tied for first place in the race.

**How much?** ***Example:*** Is there ***enough*** bread?

**Whose?** ***Example:*** ***Linda's*** dog ran away.

Finally, adjectives can also come **after** "be – verb"(am, are, is, was, and were).

***Examples:*** She is *cute*.

I am *smart*.

The king was *diligent*.

## Pattern Practice 1:

Circle the adjective and underline the noun it modifies in the sentences below.

1. Elizabeth has an elderly father.
2. The basketball player is tall.
3. The children are young.
4. The man is so muscular.
5. That girl is very short.
6. These two black pens do not have ink.
7. The lazy children failed their exam.
8. The diligent chef served the chubby customer.
9. Joseph ate the cold pizza in the morning.
10. The windy weather leads to many fallen trees.

## Grammar Focus 2: Adjectives that describe people using appearance (외모) and character (성격).

When we describe a person's physical appearance, there are two general sentence constructions using the verbs "***to be***" (am, are, is, was, and were) and "***to have***" (has, have).

***Examples:*** She ***is*** attractive. She ***has*** big, brown eyes.

Use "***to have***" (have, has, had) if you are describing part of the body.
For example, you can draw a beard or a mustache separately from a person's face. So, you would say, "He has a beard" or "She has blue eyes."

Use "***to be***" (am, are, is, was, were) if you are describing the entire body.
For example, you can't draw someone being tall or short separate from their body. So, you would say, "He is tall" or "She was short."

* We use the "be-verb" when using the word bald.
***Example:*** He is bald.

## Pattern Practice 2:

Fill in blanks using ***is*** or ***has***.

***Example:*** She ***is*** an adult. She ***is*** tall, slim and beautiful. She ***has*** long, straight, black hair.

1. He _______ of average height and average build. He _______ short, red hair. He _______ handsome.
2. She _______ really cute. She _______ medium length wavy hair and she _______ big beautiful eyes.
3. He _______ blue eyes and gray hair. He _______ about 40 years old. He _______ middle-aged. He _______quite attractive.
4. She _______ around 60. She _______ short curly hair, and wears glasses.
5. He _______ a wide face and dark skin. He _______very muscular.

## Grammar Focus 3:

### What does (s)he look like? (Appearance 외모)

This question asks about a person's appearance or physical characteristics.
It asks for a description of how someone looks.
For example, if you ask this question, someone might answer with details about the person's hair color, height, weight, facial features, etc.

### What is (s)he like? (Character 성격)

This question asks about a person's personality or character.
It asks what kind of person someone is on the inside.
For example, if you ask this question, someone might answer with information about whether the person is kind, funny, shy, outgoing, intelligent, lazy, etc.

## Dialogue (Listening and Speaking):

Listen to the dialogue and fill in the missing words. Then practice the dialogue with your partner twice.

| | |
|---|---|
| **Jane:** | Did you see the new **neighbor**? She just moved into the townhouse and her name is Mrs. Sandra Johnson. |
| **Cathy:** | You mean the lady that is (1) ________________ and (2) ________________. |
| **Jane:** | Yes. That's her. She has (3) ____________________ hair and wears it in two **pigtails** with two yellow ribbons. |
| **Cathy:** | She would be **attractive**, but she looks so (4) __________________ all the time. |
| **Jane:** | Don't be **fooled** by the way she looks. I talked to her and she is very friendly and funny. |
| **Cathy:** | Really? She looks (5) ____________________ to me. |
| **Jane:** | How old is she? |
| **Cathy:** | I'm not sure, but I would guess she is not (6) ________________. |
| **Jane:** | Yes. She's not old, but too young to be (7) ____________________. |
| **Cathy:** | What do they call people who are between young and elderly? |
| **Jane:** | I'm not sure, but I think they call people like that **middle-aged**. |

**Key Words:** neighbor 이웃사람 / pigtails 양갈래머리 / attractive 매력적인 / fooled 속은 / middle-aged 중년의

## Reading: Read the following story and then answer the questions.

### Our Family's Story

Our family is a mix of different **characters** and **appearances**.

Sarah is my aunt. She's nice, funny, and always takes care of everyone.

She's not very tall, but she has curly **brunette** hair and brown eyes. Then there's my uncle. He is tall and has a big beard. He has blue eyes.

My cousins are interesting too. One of them, Greg, looks like my aunt. He has curly brown hair and green eyes. He is **humorous** and always makes us laugh. The youngest child has wavy brown hair and is **patient**. Our older **cousin** is very strong. He is muscular and has curly hair.

I think we have a good-looking family, and we are all **diligent**.

**Key Words:** characters 성격 / appearances 외모 / brunette 갈색 머리 / humorous 유머러스한 / patient 인내심 있는 / cousin 사촌 / diligent 근면한

## Reading Questions:

1. Who is nice, funny, and always takes care of everyone?

___

2. What does Sarah look like?

___

3. What is Greg like?

___

4. What does the youngest child look like?

___

5. What is everyone in the family like?

___

## Conversation Practice 1: Ask and answer the questions with a partner.

1. What does she look like?

______________________________________

2. What does he look like?

______________________________________

3. What's he like?

______________________________________

4. What's she like?

______________________________________

**Conversation Practice 2:** Work together with a partner. You describe a famous person without saying his/her name. Then your partner guesses who this person is.

*Example:*

He is old.

He has wavy, dark brown hair.

He also has a mustache and a small beard.

He has a thin face and a light complexion.

He usually wears stylish glasses.

He is talented, charismatic, and charming.

He is loved by fans all over the world.

He was an actor in many blockbuster films including *Ironman*.

Who is he? He is Robert Downey Jr.

**Editing:** Find and correct the errors in the following sentences.

1. He has short and has black hair.

2. My father is chubby and has bald.

3. My best friend is petite and has patient.

4. Jennifer is attractive and slim, but she has stubborn.

5. The men has long beards and mustaches.

Unit **04**

# Which is bigger?

**Warm-up:** Which do you like better? Explain your reasons to your partner.

1.

OR

2.

OR

3.

OR

## Vocabulary: Technology

Match each entertainment word to a description below.

a. ___ app
b. ___ website
c. ___ laptop
d. ___ charger
e. ___ printer
f. ___ search engine
g. ___ file
h. ___ settings
i. ___ notification
j. ___ wireless

1. A ________________________ is a small computer you can carry.
2. The office needs a ________________________ for scanning and printing.
3. You can watch your Cyber Campus lessons on the Shingu College app or ____________________.
4. I downloaded a new ________________________ on my phone.
5. You can change the sound in the ____________________ of your phone.
6. Did you get a __________________________ about the meeting?
7. The new headphones connect to your phone through _________________ technology.
8. I use a ____________________________ to find information online.
9. I forgot my phone ________________________ and I have little battery.
10. Remember to save the _____________________ when you finish your work.

## Grammar Focus 1 (Comparatives 비교급): We use comparatives to compare two or more things and see how they are different from each other.

We use "*than*" when comparing two things.

**1)** For most one-syllable adjectives, we add *-er* to the adjective followed by **than.**

*Example: (tall)* Pamela is ***taller than*** Monica.

**2)** For most adjectives with two more syllables, we add **more** before the word and **than** after the word.

*Example: (beautiful)* Cinderella is ***more beautiful than*** Snow White.

## Pattern Practice 1:

Write the correct comparative form of each adjective for the sentences below. Be sure to include the word "*than*" after the comparative forms.

1. A printer is ______________________ a laptop. **(cheap)**
2. The Daewoo Matiz is much ______________________ the Hyundai Genesis. **(small)**
3. The new AI system ______________________ the old model. **(intelligent)**
4. Summer is much ______________________ winter. **(warm)**
5. Good health is ______________________ having a lot of money. **(important)**
6. Cats are ______________________ dogs. **(quiet)**
7. PSY is ______________________ Jae suk Yoo. **(young)**
8. Gold is ______________________ silver. **(expensive)**
9. The rabbit was ______________________ the turtle. **(slow)**
10. Business class is ______________________ economy class. **(comfortable)**

## Grammar Focus 2: Comparative adjectives that end in –*y* and irregular adjectives

**1)** For adjectives that end in ***y***, we drop the ***y*** and add ***ier*** followed by ***than***.

***Example:*** (pretty) Sleeping Beauty is ***prettier than*** Princess Jasmine.

**2)** Irregular adjectives

| Adjective (형용사) | Comparative form (비교급) |
|---|---|
| good | better than |
| bad | worse than |
| little | less than |
| many | more than |
| far | farther than |

## Pattern Practice 2:

Complete the sentences by writing the correct comparative form for each adjective.

1. Studying with friends is ______________________ studying alone. **(good)**
2. The distance to the Sun is ______________ the distance to the Moon. **(far)**
3. Electronic Dance Music is ___________________ classical music. **(noisy)**
4. Rio de Janeiro is _______________________ Moscow. **(sunny)**
5. One hundred kilograms is ________________ one hundred grams. **(many)**
6. One thousand cents is ____________________ twenty dollars. **(little)**
7. This cheese is ____________________ milk. **(smelly)**
8. Your room is _____________________ my room. **(messy)**
9. The cake tasted ____________________ the salad. **(bad)**
10. Roses are _____________________ sunflowers. **(lovely)**

## Pattern Practice 3:

Complete the sentences by writing the correct comparative form for each adjective.

1. Becky is ______________________ Wendy. **(old)**
2. Your job is hard but my job is much ______________________ yours. **(hard)**
3. Henry is ______________________ Dillon. **(nice)**
4. Old wines are usually ______________________ new wines. **(expensive)**
5. Phil's English is improving. It's ______________________ it was before. **(good)**
6. Most people think math is ______________________ gym. **(difficult)**
7. It's a long way from Seoul to New York, but Seoul to Paris is even ______________________ that. **(far)**
8. George leaves his house ______________________ his sister. **(early)**
9. French is a beautiful language, but I think that English is ______________________ French for our everyday lives. **(useful)**
10. African elephants are typically ______________________ Asian elephants. **(big)**

## Dialogue (Listening and Speaking):

Listen to the dialogue and fill in the missing words. Then practice the dialogue with your partner twice.

| | |
|---|---|
| **Beth:** | Hey, Greg! Did you see my new smartphone? |
| **Greg:** | No, I didn't. How does it look? |
| **Beth:** | It's great! It's (1) ____________________ my old phone, but it works much faster! |
| **Greg:** | Oh, really? My sister just got a new laptop, and she says it's (2) ______________ __________ her old one. |
| **Beth:** | Wow, that's **awesome**! I want a laptop. They seem more **useful** than smartphones. |
| **Greg:** | Yeah, they are. I think smartphones are **handier** for everyday life, like checking emails or using social media. |
| **Beth:** | True. Typing on a laptop is (3) ____________________ on my phone. Plus, the screen is (4) _______________, so it's better for watching videos. |
| **Greg:** | That's a good point. |
| **Beth:** | Anyway, I'm thinking of getting a new tablet too. I compared different models online, but I can't decide which one to get. |
| **Greg:** | Well, let me know if you need any help. I can help you (5) _______________ the **features** and prices. |
| **Beth:** | Thanks, Greg! |
| **Greg:** | No problem. Anytime! |

**Key Words:** awesome 멋진 / useful 유용한 / handier 더 편리한 / features 특징

**Reading:** Read the following story and then answer the questions.

### The Internet

The Internet is a big web. It **connects** people and **information** all around the world.

A long time ago, people used phones and letters to communicate with each other. It was slower than sending messages online today.

In the 1960s, scientists started a small club. The computers from the club could talk to each other. It was smaller than today's Internet, but it was the start. It helped **researchers** share information.

In the 1980s, the Internet got bigger. It connected more computers together. People could send emails and share files.

By the 1990s, the Internet was really growing. It became more **popular**. Everyone wanted to be online!

Today, the Internet is like a giant library. You can find anything you want. It's really important because it helps us learn and work every day.
The Internet is bigger, faster, and more important than when it started.

**Key Words:** connects 연결하다 / information 정보 / researchers 연구자들 / popular 인기 있는

## Reading Questions:

1. What is the Internet?

______________________________

2. How did people communicate with each other a long time ago?

______________________________

3. When did scientists start a small club for computers to talk to each other?

______________________________

4. What happened to the Internet in the 1980s?

______________________________

5. Is the Internet really powerful today?

______________________________

## Conversation Practice:

Work together with a partner. You make comparative questions, then your partner answers them.

***Example)*** Which is bigger, an apple or a watermelon?

*A watermelon is bigger than an apple.*

**1.** ______________________________________________?

______________________________________________

**2.** ______________________________________________?

______________________________________________

**3.** ______________________________________________?

______________________________________________

**4.** ______________________________________________?

______________________________________________

**5.** ______________________________________________?

______________________________________________

**6.** ______________________________________________?

______________________________________________

**7.** ______________________________________________?

______________________________________________

**8.** ______________________________________________?

______________________________________________

**Editing:** Find and correct the errors in the following sentences.

1. Terry runs more faster than Michael.

2. My friend is badder than me in singing.

3. This class is interestinger than my other classes.

4. The boys are taller girls in the class.

5. Summer is more hot than winter.

Unit 05

# What is the fastest?

## Warm up:

**1.** Which is the fastest way to travel?

**2.** Which is the biggest item?

**3.** Who is the tallest student in your class?

## Vocabulary 1:

Match each picture to a travel word below.

a. 

b. 

c. 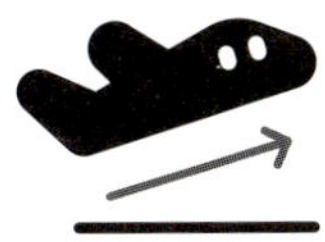

d. 

e. 

f. 

g. 

h. 

i. 

j. 

1. airport: ________
2. passenger: ________
3. rental car: ________
4. departure gate: ________
5. baggage: ________
6. departure: ________
7. arrival: ________
8. passport: ________
9. check – in counter: ________
10. reservation: ________

## Grammar Focus 1: Comparative adjectives and Superlative adjectives (비교급 형용사와 최상급 형용사)

Comparative adjectives help us compare two or more things.

We use superlative adjectives to compare three or more things. They help us show which thing is the highest or lowest in a group. If we want to say something is the most or the least, we use superlative adjectives.

When we use superlative adjectives, we usually add "***the***" in front of them. For example, we say "***the best***", "***the most***", "***the sweetest***", and so on.

1)

| | Comparative (비교급) | Superlative (최상급) |
|---|---|---|
| Most one syllable adjectives | Add -***er*** to the adjective followed by than | Add -***est*** to the adjective |
| Example using fast | Flying is faster than driving | Flying is the fastest way to travel |

2)

| | Comparative (비교급) | Superlative (최상급) |
|---|---|---|
| Most adjectives with 2 or more syllables | Add "***more***" before the word and "***than***" after the word | Add "***most***" before the word |
| Example using expensive | Air travel is more expensive than rail travel | Air travel is the most expensive form of travel |

## Pattern Practice 1:

Write the correct *comparative and superlative form* of each adjective in the table below.

| Adjective (형용사) | Comparative (비교급) | Superlative (최상급) |
|---|---|---|
| 1. young | *younger than* | *the youngest* |
| 2. intelligent | | |
| 3. warm | | |
| 4. important | | |
| 5. quiet | | |
| 6. cheap | | |
| 7. slow | | |
| 8. comfortable | | |
| 9. expensive | | |
| 10. small | | |

## Grammar Focus 2: Comparative and superlative adjectives that end in *-y* and irregular adjectives

1)

| | Comparative (비교급) | Superlative (최상급) |
|---|---|---|
| Adjectives that end in *-y* | Drop the "*y*" and add *-ier* followed by ***than*** | Drop the "*y*" and add *-iest* to the adjective |
| Example using foggy | London is foggier than Buenos Aires. | St. John's, Newfoundland is the foggiest city in North America |

2) Irregular Adjectives

| Adjective (형용사) | Comparative (비교급) | Superlative (최상급) |
|---|---|---|
| good | better than | the best |
| bad | worse than | the worst |
| little | less than | the least |
| many | more than | the most |
| far | farther than | the farthest |

## Pattern Practice 2:

Write the correct *comparative and superlative form* of each adjective in the table below.

| Adjective (형용사) | Comparative (비교급) | Superlative (최상급) |
|---|---|---|
| 1. messy | *messier than* | *the messiest* |
| 2. many | | |
| 3. sunny | | |
| 4. bad | | |
| 5. smelly | | |
| 6. good | | |
| 7. far | | |
| 8. little | | |
| 9. noisy | | |
| 10. lovely | | |

## Vocabulary 2:

Match each word to its Korean meaning.

1. beach
2. temple
3. carry – on luggage
4. souvenir
5. reception desk
6. travel agency
7. book
8. map
9. accommodation
10. sightseeing

a. 절, 사원
b. 휴대용 수하물
c. 기념품
d. 해변
e. 지도
f. 여행사
g. 숙박시설
h. 관광
i. 접수처, 프런트
j. 예약하다

## Pattern Practice 3:

Write the correct *comparative and superlative form* of each adjective in the table below.

| Adjective (형용사) | Comparative (비교급) | Superlative (최상급) |
|---|---|---|
| easy | *easier than* | *the easiest* |
| 1. hard | | |
| 2. cool | | |
| 3. hot | | |
| 4. beautiful | | |
| 5. awful | | |

## Dialogue (Listening and Speaking):

Listen to the dialogue and fill in the missing words. Then practice the dialogue with your partner twice.

| | |
|---|---|
| **Travel Agent:** | Good afternoon. This is Shingu Travel Agency. How can I help you today? |
| **Customer:** | Hello. I'm interested in planning a trip to Danang in Vietnam. |
| **Travel Agent:** | **Certainly**! When are you planning to travel? |
| **Customer:** | I want to go in the middle of January. |
| **Travel Agent:** | How many (1) ______________________ will be traveling? |
| **Customer:** | It'll just be me. |
| **Travel Agent:** | Great! We have (2) _________ ______________________ price for **accommodations** near the beach. The Hyatt is (3) _____________ __________________ resort in Danang. Would you like to book this package? |
| **Customer:** | That sounds perfect! |
| **Travel Agent:** | Excellent! The package also includes a (4) ______________ _________. So, you can easily **explore** the city and enjoy (5) _________ ______________ beautiful **sights**. |
| **Customer:** | Wonderful! Thank you for your help. |

**Key Words:** certainly 물론입니다 / accommodations 숙소 / explore 탐험하다 / sights 명소들

**Reading:** Read the following story and then answer the questions.



### East Asia

Japan, China, and Thailand are three amazing places to visit in **East Asia.**

Japan is famous for its fast trains, beautiful **cherry blossoms** in spring, and colorful leaves in **autumn.** It's the closest country for Koreans to visit from South Korea. Many **tourists** enjoy eating sushi, ramen, udon, and steak in Japan.

The Great Wall of China is very famous, old, and big. Shanghai is the busiest city in China. People travel to Shanghai to try new foods. Tourists can shop for many different kinds of souvenirs.

The people of Thailand are very friendly. You can explore busy markets in Bangkok, visit **ancient temples**, or relax on beautiful beaches. Sometimes Thailand is the best option for many Koreans. There are many cheap accommodations and activities.

Japan, China, and Thailand have lots of interesting things to do and see. If you like history, nature, or just relaxing, you'll find something you love in these countries.

**Key Words:** East Asia 동아시아 / cherry blossoms 벚꽃 / autumn 가을 / tourists 관광객 / ancient temples 고대 사원

## Reading Questions:

1. What is Japan famous for in autumn?

______________________________

2. Which country is the closest for Koreans to visit?

______________________________

3. What is famous in China?

______________________________

4. Why do people travel to Shanghai?

______________________________

5. Which country is the best option for many Koreans?

______________________________

## Conversation Practice: Ask and answer the questions with a partner.

1. Where is the best place to visit for a holiday?

______________________________

2. What is the most expensive souvenir you bought?

______________________________

3. Where is the farthest place you traveled to from your home?

______________________________

4. What country has the most delicious food?

______________________________

5. Where is the most relaxing place to visit for a holiday?

______________________________

**Editing:** Find and correct the errors in the following sentences.

1. Lotte World Tower is the taller building in South Korea.

2. Durian is the smellyer food.

3. Russia is biggest than Canada.

4. Samsung makes the goodest phones.

5. Seoul has the many people in South Korea.

Unit 06

# Review

## Unit 01: Who is your uncle?

**Vocabulary:** Match the Korean meanings for the English words.

| | |
|---|---|
| **1.** daughter | a. 이모, 고모 |
| **2.** son | b. 할아버지 |
| **3.** niece | c. 외동 |
| **4.** nephew | d. 조카(남) |
| **5.** cousin | e. 삼촌 |
| **6.** aunt | f. 사촌 |
| **7.** uncle | g. 자녀 |
| **8.** only child | h. 아들 |
| **9.** grandfather | i. 조카(여) |
| **10.** children | j. 딸 |

**Practice 1:** Fill in the blanks with a possessive form.

my, our, your, his, her, their, its

1. You should thank Wendy. She is carrying __________ heavy luggage. **(you)**
2. Ben is __________ best friend in the classroom. **(I)**
3. Larry's pictures are exciting but __________ scores are quite bad. **(he)**
4. Sarah didn't invite me to __________ birthday party. **(she)**
5. Veronica is telling __________ parents about the first day at school. **(she)**
6. My cousins phoned me from __________ house in Incheon. **(they)**
7. Julia and I decided to have a barbecue in __________ garden. **(we)**
8. The cat licked __________ paw after eating dinner. **(it)**

**Practice 2:** Fill in the blanks with a possessive pronoun.

mine, ours, yours, his, hers, theirs

1. Rosa's eyes are green? What about ______________? **(you)**
2. The jacket belongs to Paul, It's ____________. **(he)**
3. I have read a new novel. Has Sonia read ______________? **(she)**
4. Helen made her bed but her brother hasn't made ____________. **(he)**
5. I sold my bike so this money is ______________. **(I)**
6. John missed the school bus but Nancy didn't miss ______________. **(she)**
7. Can you lend me your red pen? I don't know where is ______________. **(I)**
8. Ryan, should we go in my car or ___________________. **(you)**
9. Those are the children's toys. They are ________________. **(they)**
10. That motorbike belongs to my grandfather. It's ________________. **(he)**

## Unit 02: Is there a coffee shop?

**Vocabulary:** Write the English words for the Korean meanings.

**1.** 커피숍 ______________________

**2.** 사무실 ______________________

**3.** 서점 ______________________

**4.** 식당 ______________________

**5.** 학과 사무실 ______________________

**6.** 편의점 ______________________

**7.** 체육관 ______________________

**8.** 사물함 ______________________

**Practice 1:** Fill in the blanks using ***There is***, ***There are***, ***There was***, or ***There were***.

**1.** ______________________ a big library near my house.

**2.** ______________________ a new gym in town.

**3.** ______________________ many convenience stores.

**4.** ______________________ a beautiful sunset two days ago.

**5.** ______________________ many people at the park yesterday.

**6.** ______________________ nice coffee shops when we traveled in Australia.

**Practice 2:** Fill in the blanks using ***Is there***, ***Are there***, ***Was there***, or ***Were there***.

1. ______________________ many people at the concert last night?
2. ______________________ an amusement park when you traveled last year?
3. ______________________ any good restaurants when you were in Paris?
4. ______________________ a hospital near school?
5. ______________________ any convenience stores near your house?
6. ______________________ a good place to watch the sunrise here?

**Dialogue:** Listen to the dialogue and answer the questions.

| |
|---|
| Tom: Hi Sara! You look lost. |
| Sara: Is there a new library on campus? |
| Tom: Yes, there is a new library in the main building next to the soccer field. |
| Sara: Oh, is it in that building? What's it like? |
| Tom: There's a big study area on the first floor and there are private rooms too. |
| Sara: That sounds like a good place to study. Was it **crowded**? |
| Tom: No, it wasn't. There were many seats. |
| Sara: Awesome! And were there any loud noises? |
| Tom: No, there weren't. They made it quiet. |
| Sara: Great! Do you want to go with me? |
| Tom: Yeah! Let's go together after our last class. |

**Key Words:** crowded 붐비다

## Dialogue Questions:

1. Where is the new library?

   a. It's next to the cafeteria.
   b. It's far from campus.
   c. It's next to the soccer field.
   d. It's not finished.

2. What's the library like?

   a. small and dirty
   b. big with many seats
   c. not crowded and quiet
   d. dark and noisy

3. When will they go to the library?

   a. before class
   b. after class
   c. tomorrow
   d. next week

## Unit 03: What's he like?

**Vocabulary 1:** Match the English appearance words with the Korean meanings.

| | |
|---|---|
| **1.** ___ muscular | a. 키가 큰 |
| **2.** ___ petite | b. 잘생긴 |
| **3.** ___ slim | c. 연로한 |
| **4.** ___ chubby | d. 근육질 |
| **5.** ___ tall | e. 젊은 |
| **6.** ___ short | f. 예쁜 |
| **7.** ___ handsome | g. 통통한 |
| **8.** ___ pretty | h. 날씬한 |
| **9.** ___ elderly | i. 키가 작은 |
| **10.** ___ young | j. 작은 |

**Vocabulary 2:** Match the English character words with the Korean meanings.

| | |
|---|---|
| **1.** ___ shy | a. 게으른 |
| **2.** ___ friendly | b. 친근한 |
| **3.** ___ smart | c. 믿을 수 있는 |
| **4.** ___ lazy | d. 고집스러운 |
| **5.** ___ funny | e. 똑똑한 |
| **6.** ___ serious | f. 인내심 있는 |
| **7.** ___ diligent | g. 재미있는 |
| **8.** ___ stubborn | h. 부지런한 |
| **9.** ___ patient | i. 수줍은 |
| **10.** ___ reliable | j. 진지한 |

## **Practice 1:** Choose **is** or **has.**

1. Maria _______ attractive. She _______ big, brown eyes.
2. John _______ blue eyes and gray hair. He _______ middle-aged.
3. She _______ an adult. She _______ tall and beautiful. She _______ long, black hair.
4. He _______ of average height. He _______ short, red hair. He _______ handsome.

## **Dialogue:** Listen to the dialogue and answer the questions.

**Andrea:** Did you see the new neighbor? He just moved in next door, and his name is Miles Davis.

**Lana:** You mean the guy who's tall and chubby?

**Andrea:** Yes, exactly. He has short blonde hair and has a beard and mustache.

**Lana:** He would be attractive, but he seems serious all the time.

**Andrea:** You're wrong! I had a chat with him, and he's very funny and friendly.

**Lana:** Really? He doesn't look friendly.

**Andrea:** How old is he?

**Lana:** I'm not sure, but I think he's not too young.

**Andrea:** I think you're right. He's not young or elderly.

**Lana:** What's the word for people who are in between young and old?

**Andrea:** I think the word you are looking for is middle-aged.

## Dialogue Questions:

1. What is Miles Davis' character?

a. He is funny.
b. He is serious.
c. He is shy.
d. He is boring.

2. What does he look like?

a. petite with blonde hair
b. tall with dark hair
c. medium height, slim, with red hair
d. tall, chubby, with blonde hair

3. How old is he?

a. young
b. middle aged
c. elderly
d. teenager

## Unit 04: Which is bigger?

**Vocabulary:** Match the Korean meanings for the English words.

| | |
|---|---|
| **1.** ___ app | a. 노트북 |
| **2.** ___ website | b. 프린터 |
| **3.** ___ laptop | c. 충전기 |
| **4.** ___ charger | d. 파일 |
| **5.** ___ printer | e. 앱 |
| **6.** ___ search engine | f. 설정 |
| **7.** ___ file | g. 알림 |
| **8.** ___ settings | h. 무선 |
| **9.** ___ notification | i. 웹사이트 |
| **10.** ___ wireless | j. 검색 엔진 |

**Practice:** Fill in the blanks with the correct comparative form.

***Example:*** Sarah is _*more beautiful than*_ ***(beautiful)*** her friend.

**1.** Summer is ______________________________ **(hot)** winter.

**2.** The blue car is ______________________________ **(expensive)** the green one.

**3.** This restaurant has ______________________________ **(good)** food the one we tried last time.

**4.** Today is ______________________________ **(sunny)** it was yesterday.

5. This movie is ______________________________ **(exciting)** the one we watched last week.

6. My house is ______________________________ **(far)** yours.

7. My dog is ______________________________ **(friendly)** the neighbor's dog.

8. The movie we watched yesterday was ______________________ **(bad)** we expected.

**Reading:** Read the following story and then answer the questions.

### Video Games

Video games changed a lot over time. It is more exciting for players.

In the beginning, video games were simple. Games like Super Mario Bros. and Pac-Man were popular on early **game consoles.**

As technology **improved**, so did video games. Consoles like the Nintendo and Sega Genesis brought better graphics and more fun games to players' homes. In the 1990s, video games started using 3D graphics, and it made them look even cooler. Games like Super Mario 64 and Sonic the Hedgehog amazed players with their worlds and gameplay.

Today, video games are everywhere. People can play games on their phones, computers, and consoles. Games like Candy Crush and Among Us are popular with players of all ages.

**Key Words:** game console 게임기 / improved 개선된

## Reading Questions:

1. Which game was popular in the early days of video gaming?

   a. Super Mario Bros.
   b. Minecraft
   c. Candy Crush
   d. Among Us

2. What made games like Super Mario 64 and Sonic the Hedgehog cool in the 1990s?

   a. 2D graphics
   b. online gaming
   c. 3D graphics
   d. mobile gaming

3. How has gaming changed today?

   a. People can only play on consoles.
   b. Games are less fun than before.
   c. People can play on phones, computers, and consoles.
   d. Games are only popular with kids.

## Unit 05: What is the fastest?

**Vocabulary:** Match the Korean meanings for the English words.

| | | |
|---|---|---|
| 1. ______ passenger | | a. 도착 |
| 2. ______ departure gate | | b. 출발 |
| 3. ______ baggage | | c. 예약 |
| 4. ______ departure | | d. 예약하다 |
| 5. ______ arrival | | e. 승객 |
| 6. ______ passport | | f. 기념품 |
| 7. ______ reservation | | g. 숙박 |
| 8. ______ carry – on luggage | | h. 수하물 |
| 9. ______ souvenir | | i. 휴대용 수하물 |
| 10. ______ book | | j. 관광 |
| 11. ______ accommodation | | k. 여권 |
| 12. ______ sightseeing | | l. 출발 게이트 |

**Practice:** Write the correct comparative and superlative forms of the adjective in the table.

| Adjective (형용사) | Comparative form (비교급) | Superlative form (최상급) |
|---|---|---|
| warm | | |
| bad | | |
| important | | |
| sunny | | |
| slow | | |
| expensive | | |
| hot | | |
| far | | |
| easy | | |

**Reading:** Read the following story and then answer the questions.

### Famous Landmarks

All over the world, there are many famous **landmarks**. They amaze people.

The Eiffel Tower in Paris, France, is one of the most famous landmarks. It is a symbol of romance and beauty and has beautiful views of the city.

In Egypt, the Great Pyramids of Giza are the oldest and most interesting landmarks.

The **Statue** of **Liberty** in New York City is one of the most **welcoming** symbols of the United States. The Statue of Liberty is a sign of **freedom**.

In Rio de Janeiro, Brazil, Christ the **Redeemer** is the tallest statue. It shows us the city's prettiest views.

Many people visit and love these landmarks.

**Key Words:** landmarks 눈에 띄는 큰 건축물 / statue 동상 / liberty, freedom 자유 / welcoming 환영하는 / redeemer 구세주

## Reading Questions:

1. What is the Eiffel Tower a symbol of?

   a. adventure and excitement
   b. peace and harmony
   c. power and strength
   d. romance and beauty

2. What is the Statue of Liberty a sign of?

   a. friendship
   b. freedom
   c. money
   d. power

3. What is the tallest statue in Brazil?

   a. Christ the Redeemer
   b. The Great Pyramids of Giza
   c. The Statue of Liberty
   d. The Eiffel Tower

Unit 07

# Does she like jazz or pop?

**Warm-up:** What kind of music do you like?

Name three types of music you like.

________________ ________________ ________________

Name three types of music you don't like.

________________ ________________ ________________

## Vocabulary 1: Music Genres

| | | | |
|---|---|---|---|
| genre | pop | hip-hop | classical |
| jazz | R&B | electronic | rock |
| Latin | reggae | ballad | country |

## Grammar Focus 1: Conjunctions (접속사)

Conjunctions are joining words. The purpose of a conjunction is to link together two parts of a sentence. Conjunctions have different functions. Here are some of them with their conjunction words.

| Conjunction (접속사) | Function (기능) | Example |
|---|---|---|
| and (그리고) | addition (추가) | I like jazz and rock music. |
| but (그러나) | contrast (대조) | I like pop but hate country music. |
| or (또는) | alternatives (선택) | I want to listen to R&B or hip-hop. |

## Pattern Practice 1: Fill in the blanks using ***or***, ***but***, or ***and***.

***Example:*** He can sing _and_ dance very well.

1. I want to go to the park, __________ it's raining outside.
2. She likes apples __________ oranges.
3. Do you like tea __________ coffee?
4. He is tall __________ strong.
5. We can go to the beach, __________ we can stay home.
6. The cake is delicious, __________ it's too sweet.
7. You can have chocolate __________ vanilla ice cream.
8. She is smart __________ kind.
9. I called you, __________ you didn't answer.
10. Do you want to go now __________ later?

## Grammar Focus 2: Conjunctions (접속사)

| Conjunction (접속사) | Function (기능) | Example |
|---|---|---|
| because (…때문에) | reason/cause (이유) | I like electronic music because it's perfect for dancing |
| so (그래서) | result (결과) | It's perfect for dancing so I like electronic music. |

***Examples:***

I was tired _so_ I went to bed. I went to bed _because_ I was tired.

*(first)* → *(then)* *(then)* → *(first)*

## Pattern Practice 2: Fill in the blanks using ***because*** or ***so***.

***Example:*** It's great for working out _so_ I like electronic music.

1. I missed the bus ____________ I was late.
2. She is tired ____________ she didn't sleep well.
3. We stayed inside ____________ it was raining.
4. He is happy ____________ he got a new job.
5. They are excited ____________ they are going on vacation.
6. They are going on vacation ____________ they are excited.
7. She wants to pass the exam ____________ she is studying hard.
8. The soup is hot ____________ it just came off the stove.
9. The kids are playing outside ____________ the weather is nice.
10. It might rain ____________ he brought an umbrella.

## Pattern Practice 3: Complete the sentences using **and**, ***or***, ***but***, ***so***, or ***because***.

***Example:*** It's great for working out _so_ I like electronic music.

1. I went to the store _____ I forgot to buy milk.
2. She loves to read books ______ watch movies.
3. He studied all night ______ he passed the exam.
4. We can go to the park _______ we can visit the museum.
5. They wanted to watch a movie ______ it was sold out.
6. I like to swim _____ I joined the swimming team.
7. She was hungry ______ she didn't eat breakfast.
8. We were tired ______ we went to bed early.
9. He plays the guitar ______ he sings.
10. Bring your jacket ______ it's cold outside.

## Dialogue (Listening and Speaking):

Listen to the dialogue and fill in the missing words. Then practice the dialogue with your partner twice.

| | |
|---|---|
| Arthur: | Hi Jackie! Do you like listening to music (1) ______________ playing games? |
| Jackie: | I love listening to music! There are so many different types of music. |
| Arthur: | I know, right? I like listening to classical music (2) ____________________ it's **soothing**. |
| Jackie: | Oh, I **prefer** listening to hip-hop music because it has a great beat. |
| Arthur: | Hip-hop music is cool, (3) ____________________ I also enjoy listening to country music because of the stories in the songs. |
| Jackie: | That's interesting! Country music is nice, but I like to dance, (4) ____________________ I like listening to electronic music. |
| Arthur: | Electronic dance music is fun! So, what's your favorite music genre? |
| Jackie: | It's hard to pick just one, but I think I like hip-hop music the best because it's really **catchy**. How about you? |
| Arthur: | I like classical music the most because it helps me relax (5) ____________________ focus. |
| Jackie: | That's great! It's cool how we can enjoy different types of music. |
| Arthur: | **Definitely**! Music makes people happy in many ways. |

**Key Words:** soothing 마음을 달래주는 / prefer 선호하다 / catchy 기억하기 쉬운 / definitely 확실히, 분명히

**Reading:** Read the following story and then answer the questions.

### Black Pink

Blackpink is a famous girl group from South Korea. They sing fun songs and dance with a lot of energy.

The group has four members: Jisoo, Jennie, Rose, and Lisa. Each member has their own style, but they work together to make great music.

Blackpink's music is a mix of pop, hip-hop, and dance. Their songs are catchy and often talk about love and **confidence**. Some of their most popular songs are "Ddu-Du Ddu-Du", "Kill This Love", and "How You Like That".

They are busy, but Blackpink always makes time for their fans. They talk to their fans on social media and have concerts all over the world. They really care about their fans and are thankful for their **support**.

Blackpink is a talented girl group and has fans all over the world. They make great music, dance well, and love their fans a lot.

**Key words:** confidence 자신감 / support 지원

## Reading Questions:

1. Is BlackPink a boy group?

 ______________________________

2. How many members does BlackPink have?

 ______________________________

3. What type of music do they sing?

 ______________________________

4. What do their songs often talk about?

 ______________________________

5. Do Blackpink members talk to their fans?

 ______________________________

## Conversation Practice: Ask and answer the questions with a partner.

1. What music genres make you feel happy?
2. What music genres make you feel sad?
3. What music genres make you feel energetic?
4. Do you prefer to listen to music alone, or do you share your favorite songs with friends?
5. How do you discover new music, and do you have any artists you like?

**Editing:** Find and correct the errors in the following sentences.

1. I like to listen to jazz music, or I don't like rock music.

2. I was late for school and I got up late.

3. He wanted to play soccer because he called his friend to join him.

4. We can eat Chinese food but Italian food for lunch.

5. They can enjoy the concert because eat dinner together afterwards.

Unit 08

# What would you like to order?

## Warm-up:

Let's make a sandwich! Choose ingredients (재료) from the list below.

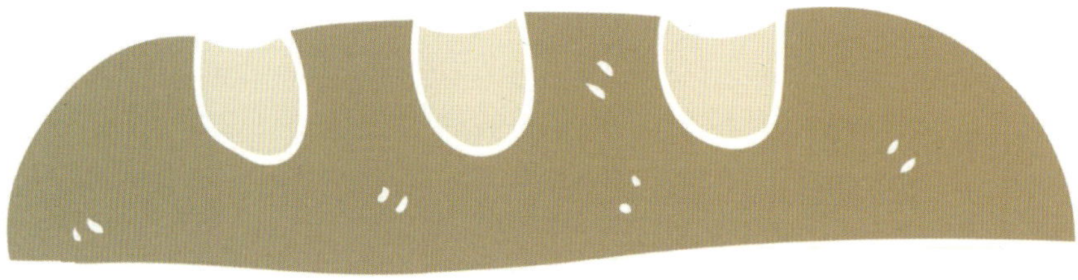

______________ ______________ ______________

______________ ______________ ______________

## Vocabulary 1:

| | | | | |
|---|---|---|---|---|
| olives | lettuce | cheese | ketchup | pickles |
| tomato | onion | cucumber | sliced egg | mayonnaise |
| salt | pepper | bacon | pepperoni | mustard |

## Vocabulary 2:

| Drinks | Dishes | Dessert |
|---|---|---|
| Espresso<br>Americano<br>Latte<br>Cappuccino<br>Decaffeinated Coffee<br>Bottled Water | Salad (Greek, Caesar)<br>Sandwiches (Turkey, Ham, Tuna)<br>Burger<br>Pizza<br>Spaghetti<br>Risotto<br>Paella<br>Pho<br>Pad Thai<br>Vegan Panini | Cake (Red Velvet, Pound, Black Forest, Carrot)<br>Apple Pie<br>Frozen Yogurt |

## Grammar Focus 1: ***May***, ***Could***, and ***Would***

| Questions | | | | Short Answers | |
|---|---|---|---|---|---|
| May/Can/Could | Subject | Base Verb | | Affirmative | Negative |
| May<br>Can<br>Could | I | ask | a question? | Of course.<br>Certainly.<br>Sure.<br>Ok.<br>No Problem. | I'm sorry, no. |
| May<br>Can<br>Could | I | help | you? | Yes, please. | No, thanks. |
| Can<br>Could<br>Would | you | help | me? | Of course.<br>Certainly.<br>Sure.<br>Ok. | No, I cannot |

We use ***May I***, ***Can I***, ***Could I*** to ask for permission or to offer help.

All three expressions have similar meanings, but they differ in terms of politeness. ***May I*** is the most polite and formal, ***Could I*** is more polite than ***Can I***, and ***Could I*** is suitable for almost all situations.

***Would you*** and ***Could you*** are polite ways to ask someone to do something and they have the same meaning. (***Can you*** is less formal. We can use ***Can you*** in casual situations.)

## Pattern practice 1a: Complete the conversations using *may*, *can*, *could*, or *would*.

1. Waiter: _*May*_ I take your order?
   Customer: No, Sorry, I am not ready.

2. Waiter: ______________ I take the plates from you?
   Customer: Sure.

3. Customer: ________________ you give me a menu?
   Waiter: Here's the menu. Just let me know if you have any questions.

4. Customer: _______________ I have some more orange juice?
   Waiter: Certainly, sir.

5. Employee: ________________ I ask a question, sir?
   CEO: Yes, of course.

## Pattern practice 1b: Rewrite the sentences in the correct order.

1. pass / Could / me / the mustard / you
   ____________________________________________________________?

2. you / carry / Could / my suitcase
   ____________________________________________________________?

3. you / would / like / What / to / order

______________________________________________?

4. I / like / to / the cherry pie / have / would

______________________________________________?

5. the restroom / I / May / use

______________________________________________?

## Grammar Focus 2: Would like (to)

<table>
<tr><th colspan="6">Statements</th></tr>
<tr><th colspan="2">Subject</th><th colspan="2">Would Like</th><th colspan="2">Object</th></tr>
<tr><td colspan="2">I<br>You<br>He<br>She<br>We<br>They</td><td colspan="2">would like<br>(‘d like)</td><td colspan="2">a glass of water.</td></tr>
<tr><td colspan="4">Yes/No Questions</td><td colspan="2">Short Answers</td></tr>
<tr><td>Would</td><td>you<br>he/she<br>they</td><td>like</td><td>a glass of water?</td><td>Yes,<br>I/we/he/she/they<br>Would.</td><td>No,<br>I/we/he/she/they<br>Wouldn’t.</td></tr>
</table>

When a verb follows “***would like***”, we use the base form of the verb with “***to***”.

**Would you like to** travel?

**I’d like to** go to Italy.

**Note:** We do not use ‘*Would I like*...?’ Or ‘*Would we like*...?’
We use ***Would like*** in place of want. ***Would like*** is more polite.

I would like a glass of water. (polite)

## Pattern practice 2: Rewrite the sentences to polite form.

***Example:*** I _want_ to drink some coffee. → I _would like_ to drink some coffee.

1. I want a glass of milk.

   ______________________________

2. She wants to see the dessert menu.

   ______________________________

3. My friend wants a slice of chocolate cake.

   ______________________________

4. We want some water.

   ______________________________

5. He wants extra cheese on his pizza.

   ______________________________

## Dialogue (Listening and Speaking):

Listen to the dialogue and fill in the missing words. Then practice the dialogue with your partner twice.

| | |
|---|---|
| Cafeteria Worker: | Welcome to Shingu Cafe! (1) __________ I take your order? |
| Customer: | (2) ______________ I have a menu, please? |
| Cafeteria Worker: | Of course, here you are. |
| Customer: | Thank you. (3) ____________ you **recommend** a good sandwich? |
| Cafeteria Worker: | Certainly, our **turkey** sandwich and **tuna** sandwich are popular. |
| Customer: | That sounds great. I'll have the turkey sandwich and I (4) ________________ a cappuccino, please. |

| | |
|---|---|
| **Cafeteria Worker:** | No problem. (5) ______________ you like anything else? |
| **Customer:** | Do you have any dessert options? |
| **Cafeteria Worker:** | Yes, we have some cakes, pies, frozen yogurt, and chocolate cake. Are you interested in any of these? |
| **Customer:** | Sounds perfect! I'll have a slice of the Chocolate Cake, please. |
| **Cafeteria Worker:** | Excellent choices! (6) ______________ you like that for here or **to go**? |
| **Customer:** | I'll take it to go, please. |
| **Cafeteria Worker:** | Your order will be ready **shortly**. Thank you! |

**Key words:** recommend 추천하다 / turkey 칠면조 / tuna 참치 / to go (포장해서) 가져가다 / shortly 곧



**Reading:** Read the following story and then answer the questions.

### Gourmet restaurants

A '맛집' is a word used in Korea. It means a restaurant that is famous for its delicious food. Nowadays, many people search online to visit these **gourmet** restaurants. Some people wait in long lines to enter these **hotspots**. Families **run** many of these restaurants, and people like their quality of food, service, and **atmosphere**. Many new restaurants open almost every day **as well**. It's a mix of old and new places. They **specialize** in a variety of **cuisines**, such as traditional Korean, Italian, Spanish, Vietnamese, and Thai food. People like these restaurants, and they often take photos to remember the space and food. Customers post their photos on their social media platforms to share their experiences with others.

**Key words:** gourmet 맛있는(음식), 미식가 / hotspots (인기 있는) 음식점, 장소 / run 운영하다 / atmosphere 분위기 / as well 또한 / specialize in ~을 전문으로 하다 / cuisines 음식

## Reading Questions:

1. What does the word '맛집' mean?

   ______________________________

2. How do people find these gourmet restaurants nowadays?

   ______________________________

3. Why do some people wait in long lines?

   ______________________________

4. What types of cuisines do restaurants specialize in?

   ______________________________

5. What do customers do with the photos they take?

   ______________________________

## Conversation Practice: Ask and answer the questions with a partner.

***Example:*** Q: What would you like to do this summer/ winter vacation?

A: I would like to go hiking in the mountains this summer vacation.

1. Q: Where would you like to go for lunch/dinner?

   A: ______________________________

2. Q: What would you like to eat?

   A: ______________________________

3. Q: When would you like to hang out with your friends?

   A: ______________________________

4. Q: Who would you like to go shopping with?

   A: ______________________________

5. Q: ______________________________?

   A: ______________________________



**Editing:** Find and correct the errors in the following sentences.

1. May you pass me the salt?

2. May I help I?

3. May you call me later?

4. May you read this?

5. May you help my sister?

Unit 09

# What should I do?

**Warm up:** How can we stay healthy? What are some good things and bad things for our health? Use the phrases below to complete the lists. Then add some of your own.

| Good Health | Bad Health |
|---|---|
| ______________________________ | ______________________________ |
| ______________________________ | ______________________________ |
| ______________________________ | ______________________________ |
| ______________________________ | ______________________________ |

| | |
|---|---|
| eat fresh vegetables | exercise every day |
| smoke cigarettes | drink lots of alcohol |
| stay up all night | eat salty snacks |
| go to sleep before 11PM | drink fresh fruit juice |

## Vocabulary 1: Body

| | | |
|---|---|---|
| ___ stomach | ___ shoulder | ___ stomach |
| ___ arm | ___ elbow | ___ hand |
| ___ head | ___ forehead | ___ cheeks |
| ___ chin | ___ neck | ___ waist |
| ___ leg | ___ calf | ___ thigh |
| ___ foot | ___ ankle | ___ heel |
| ___ knee | ___ fingers | ___ thumb |
| ___ eye | ___ teeth | ___ lips |
| ___ buttocks | ___ pelvis | ___ back |

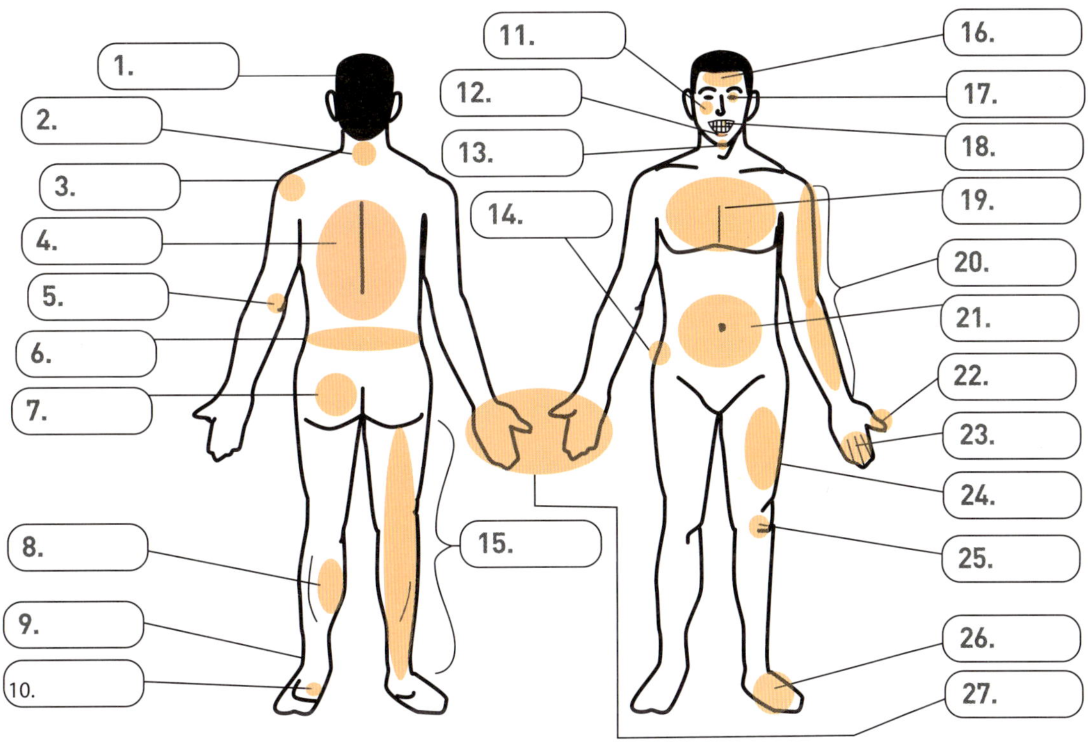

## Vocabulary 2: Health Problems

| | | |
|---|---|---|
| a headache | a stomachache | a cold |
| a toothache | dandruff | a fever |
| a sore throat | insomnia | a broken leg |

1.

____________________

2.

____________________

3.
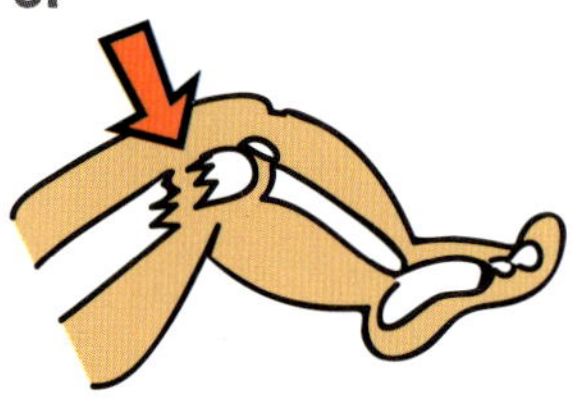

____________________

4.
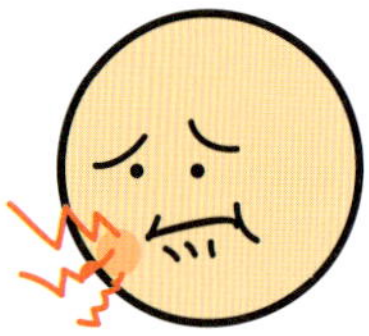

____________________

5.

____________________

6.
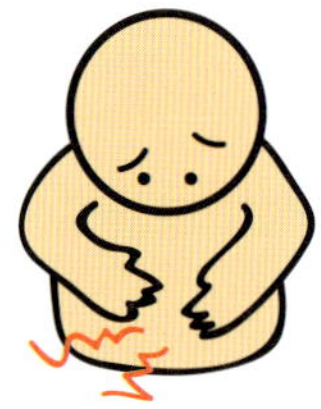

____________________

7.
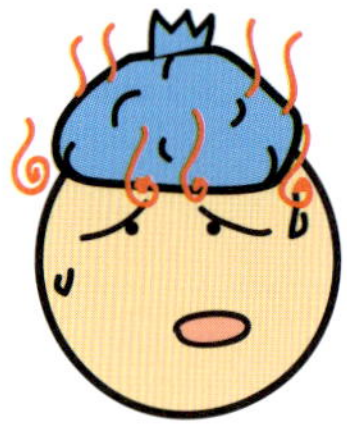

____________________

8.

____________________

9.

____________________

## Grammar Focus 1: Should I? Should, Shouldn't

We use ***should*** for suggestions **(제안)**. We use it when we think something is a good idea or the right things to do. We use this for present tense **(현재 시제)** or future tense **(미래 시제)**.

| Should I take this medicine? | Yes, you should. You should take that medicine. | No, you shouldn't. You shouldn't take that medicine. |
|---|---|---|

Here are some things we should do when we're sick. Can you match them to the health problems above? There can be more than one correct answer.

| take medicine | get some rest | take some aspirin |
|---|---|---|
| go to the emergency room | drink some warm milk | take some vitamin C |
| use special shampoo | exercise | see a doctor |
| use some ointment | drink warm fluids | take some cough drops |

## Pattern Practice 1:

Fill in the blank with ***has*** or ***have***.

1. Rebecca __________ insomnia.
2. Brian and Patrick __________ big feet.
3. Do you __________ a stomachache?
4. I __________ dandruff again.
5. Teddy __________ a fever.

## Pattern Practice 2: Health Problems

Practice speaking and writing the following patterns with new information.

***Example:*** I, headache, take some aspirin, drink lots of beer

*a.* I have a headache. What should I do?

*b.* You should take some aspirin, but you shouldn't drink lots of beer.

**1.** *Sam, stomachache, take some medicine, eat spicy food*

a. Sam has a stomachache. What should he do?

b. He should take some medicine, but he shouldn't eat spicy food.

**2.** *I, insomnia, drink warm milk, drink coffee*

a. _____ have _________________________. What should ______ do?

b. You should ____________________________________________,

but you shouldn't ____________________________________________.

**3.** *Sunny, broken arm, go to the emergency room, exercise*

a. ________ has ________________. What _________________________?

b. She should ____________________________________________,

but she shouldn't ____________________________________________.

**4.** *I, toothache, go to the dentist, drink soda*

a. _____________________________. _________________________________?

b. ____________________________________________________________,

____________________________________________________________.

**5.** *Kevin, cold, take vitamin C, go outside without a jacket*

a. _____________________________. _________________________________?

b. ____________________________________________________________,

____________________________________________________________.

Unit 09

## Dialogue (Listening and Speaking):

Listen to the dialogue and fill in the missing words. Then practice the dialogue with your partner twice.

| | |
|---|---|
| **Nancy:** | Hi James. You don't look well. What's up? |
| **James:** | Hey, I have a (1) ________________. It doesn't go away. |
| **Nancy:** | Oh no, that's not good. Maybe you (2) ________________ try to rest. |
| **James:** | I tried, but I couldn't fall asleep. |
| **Nancy:** | Hmm, did you drink any water? If you don't drink enough water, it sometimes can **cause** headaches. |
| **James:** | Yeah, I drank water, but it didn't help. |
| **Nancy:** | Well, maybe you (3) ________________ **stress** your eyes too much. Did you use your smartphone a lot? |
| **James:** | Yeah, I was watching videos on my phone. |
| **Nancy:** | Maybe you (4) ________________ **take a break** from your smartphone for a while. Also, you (5) ________________ forget to eat something. |
| **James:** | You're right. I'll try that. Thanks, Nancy. |
| **Nancy:** | No problem, James. If you're not feeling better tomorrow, you should see a doctor. |

**Key Words:** cause 유발하다 / stress 스트레스를 주다 / take a break 휴식하다

**Reading:** Read the following story and then answer the questions.

### The Lost Wallet

Emily and David should keep their wallets safe, but they didn't. They went to a **crowded** amusement park and put their **wallets** in their back pockets.

Later, when they tried to buy snacks, they **realized** their wallets were missing.

Emily's **heart sank**. She had a stomachache from losing her wallet. David's **heart raced** when he searched his pockets. He had a headache from losing his wallet.

They knew they should be **careful** with their wallets. They promised each other to always keep their wallets in a safe place from now on.

Now Emily and David are more careful with their **belongings**. They always keep their wallets in their bags or front pockets. They also make sure to often check their pockets. They learned their lesson.

**Key Words:** crowded 혼잡한 / wallets 지갑 / realized 깨달았다 / heart sank 가슴이 철렁했다 / heart raced 심장이 뛰었다 / careful 조심하는 / belongings 소지품

## Reading Questions:

1. Where did Emily and David go?

2. Where did they put the wallets?

3. What health problem did Emily have?

4. What health problem did David have?

5. What did they promise each other?

## Conversation Practice: Ask and answer the questions with a partner.

1. What are two things Koreans should eat for a stomachache?

   a) ______________________

   b) ______________________

2. What are two things Koreans should drink for a sore throat?

   a) ______________________

   b) ______________________

3. When was the last time you were sick?

   ______________________

4. What was wrong?

   ______________________

5. What did you do?

   ______________________

**Editing:** Find and correct the errors in the following sentences.



1. She shouldn't eats too much candy.

2. You should drink coffee if you have insomnia.

3. She have a sore throat, so she should drink some tea.

4. You should goes to the emergency room if you have a broken leg.

5. They has headaches and should rest.

Unit 10

# What do you have to do?

## Warm-up 1: Did your professor make any rules for your class?

Talk with your partner and list the three most important ones.

1. ______________________________
2. ______________________________
3. ______________________________

Now make a list of some rules for each of the following:

| home | movie theater | driving |
|---|---|---|
| ____________ | ____________ | ____________ |
| ____________ | ____________ | ____________ |
| ____________ | ____________ | ____________ |

## Vocabulary 1: Basic Rules

Match each word to its description on page 95.

1. ___ curfew
2. ___ strict
3. ___ illegal
4. ___ forbidden
5. ___ lenient
6. ___ age limit
7. ___ legal
8. ___ allowed
9. ___ maximum
10. ___ minimum

a. The government says it's okay.

b. I'm not old enough.

c. My dad doesn't force me to study hard.

d. I have to be home by 10 PM.

e. My parents or teachers say it's okay.

f. The government says it's not okay.

g. My mother forces me to study too hard.

h. The least.

i. The most.

j. My parents or teacher say it's not okay.

## Grammar Focus 1: Should vs. Have to

We use ***should*** and ***shouldn't*** when suggesting a proper and improper action.

We use ***have to*** and ***don't have to*** when something is either required or not.

| should = a suggestion (제안) | have to = an obligation (의무) |
|---|---|
| What should I do?<br>You should get some exercise.<br><br>Should I drink more water?<br>Yes, you should. | What do you have to do?<br>I have to go to school.<br><br>Do I have to pay for lunch?<br>No, you don't. It's free. |
| **shouldn't = (하면 안 돼)** | **don't have to = (~할 필요 없다, ~해야 하는 것은 아니다)** |
| You shouldn't play cell phone games in class.<br>You shouldn't eat too much pizza. | You don't have to study Spanish in Shingu College.<br>I don't have to go to the movies. |

**Pattern Practice 1a:** Complete the sentences using ***should***, ***shouldn't***, ***have to***, or ***don't have to***.

1. a. I can't sleep at night.

   b. You ______________________ drink warm milk.

2. a. The English class is free.

   b. You ______________________ pay for it.

3. a. The bus leaves at 6AM.

   b. We ______________________ get up early.

4. a. I want to diet.

   b. You ______________________ eat a lot of pizza.

5. a. Let's go to the museum.

   b. Okay, but we ______________________ buy a ticket.

6. a. Why aren't you studying for the test?

   b. The book is easy for me, so I ______________________ study.

7. a. I can't get to sleep.

   b. You ______________________ drink so much coffee.

8. a. Can a child get a driver's license.

   b. No, you ______________________ be 16.

9. a. Is there class every day?

   b. No, you ______________________ come on weekends.

10. a. Is this a non-smoking restaurant?

    b. Yes. You ______________________ put out your cigarette.

## Pattern Practice 1b: Rewrite the sentences in the correct order.

1. has to Jennifer harder study.

______________________________________________

2. have to wear You safety work glasses to.

______________________________________________

3. careful They be more should.

______________________________________________

4. wear Bicyclists helmets should.

______________________________________________

5. nineteen have to to vote be You.

______________________________________________

## Dialogue (Listening and Speaking):

Listen to the dialogue and fill in the missing words. Then practice the dialogue with your partner twice.

| | |
|---|---|
| **Jim:** | Hey, Pam. Did you hear about the new rules for the party tonight? |
| **Pam:** | No, is there any change? |
| **Jim:** | Well, the host made a (1) ________________ for everyone. We (2) ________________ ________________ by midnight. |
| **Pam:** | Midnight? That's really early. |
| **Jim:** | Yeah, they're trying to be safe. They (3) ________________ certain age limits for the guests. People under 18 aren't allowed. |
| **Pam:** | Oh, I see. So, it's only for **legal adults** then. |
| **Jim:** | **Exactly**. And also, bringing alcohol is **forbidden**. |
| **Pam:** | Right, I heard about that. It's (4) ________________ to bring alcohol to underage parties. |
| **Jim:** | Yeah, we don't want to get in trouble. They set a maximum number of guests, so it won't get too **crowded**. |
| **Pam:** | That's good. It makes sure everyone stays safe. So, what's the minimum age to **attend**? |
| **Jim:** | You (5) ________________ **at least** 18 to go. So, I guess I'm okay to join! |
| **Pam:** | Great, then I'll see you there! |

**Key words:** legal adults 법적 성인 / exactly 정확히 / forbidden 금지된 / crowded 혼잡한 / attend 참석하다 / at least 최소한

**Reading:** Read the following story and then answer the questions.

### The Rules of Soccer

Soccer is a fun and popular sport and people all **around the world** enjoy it. Everyone has to understand the rules to play soccer.

Each team has to have 11 players on the field, **including** a goalkeeper. Only the goalkeeper can touch the ball with hands.

The main point of soccer is to score goals. Players have to kick the ball into the **opponent**'s goal to score points. Players have to **pay attention** to the offside rule. They shouldn't be in front of the opponents when their teammate passes them the ball. Players shouldn't foul during the game. Fouls can **result in** free kicks or penalty kicks for the opponent.

When the ball goes **out of bounds**, players have to use both hands to throw the ball back onto the field. This is called a throw-in.

When they understand these rules, players can have an enjoyable and fair soccer game!

**Key words:** around the world 전 세계적으로 / including 포함하여 / opponent 상대팀 / pay attention 주의하다 / result in 결과를 초래하다 / out of bounds 경계선 밖

## Reading Questions:

1. Who can touch the ball with hands?

______________________________

2. What is the main point of soccer?

______________________________

3. Do players have to pay attention to the offside rule?

______________________________

4. Should players foul?

______________________________

5. What do players have to do when the ball goes out of bounds?

______________________________

## Conversation Practice: Ask and answer the questions with a partner.

1. Do you have a curfew? If so, what is it?

______________________________

2. What are some other rules at your house?

______________________________

______________________________

______________________________

3. Who do you think our strictest teacher is?

______________________________

4. Who do you think is the most lenient?

______________________________

5. What are some new rules you would like to see for:

a. bus stops ______________________________.

b. subway cars ______________________________.

c. car drivers ______________________________.



**Editing:** Find and correct the errors in the following sentences.

1. I shouldn't stop smoking if I want to run the marathon.

2. Students have to use their phones during class.

3. I don't like the sweater so I have to buy it.

4. Students don't have to wear pajamas to school.

5. I'm only sixteen. I have to go to the army yet.

Unit 11

# Do you like spicy food?

**Warm up:** Look at the table below. Write something you love and something you hate for each category. Then compare your table with a partner.

| Category | Love | Hate |
|---|---|---|
| food | | |
| sport | | |
| movie | | |
| music | | |
| TV show | | |
| vacation spot | | |
| holiday | | |

## Vocabulary:

| | | | |
|---|---|---|---|
| genre | comedy | horror | romance |
| extreme sports | martial arts | souvenir | scenic view |
| ethnic food | food poisoning | spicy | bland |

**Word Bank**: Can you think of more words for each category?

| ethnic foods | extreme sports | movie genres | holidays |
|---|---|---|---|
| ______ | ______ | ______ | ______ |
| ______ | ______ | ______ | ______ |
| ______ | ______ | ______ | ______ |

## Grammar Focus 1: We use the following expressions to express different degrees of *like* and *dislike*:

| | |
|---|---|
| **strong like** | I love the movie Avatar! It's fantastic! |
| **like** | I like ethnic food. It's interesting to find new flavors. |
| **weak like** | K-pop is okay. I listen to it sometimes. |
| **neutral** | It's so-so. I could take it or leave it. |
| **weak dislike** | I'm not crazy about horror films. |
| **dislike** | I don't like variety shows. |
| **strong dislike** | I hate horror movies! It's too scary for me! |

## Pattern Practice 1: Complete the sentences.

***Example:*** Do you like spicy food?

*Yes, I like it. I usually eat spicy food with friends.*

1. Do you enjoy classical music?

   Yes, __________ love _______________. It's so beautiful and calming.

2. How do you feel about horror movies?

   I'm not a fan. ______ can't __________ horror movies because it's too scary.

3. Do you like Valentine's Day?

   No, __________ hate ______________. I never have a date.

4. Do you watch horror movies?

   No, _______ don't ___________ them. I get nightmares and can't sleep.

5. Do you enjoy watching sports?

   _________ okay. I could take it or leave it.

## Grammar Focus 2: Statements of agreement and disagreement.

| Statement | Agree (동의하다) | Disagree (동의하지 않다) |
|---|---|---|
| I'm going to Las Vegas. | So am I. | I'm not. |
| I was at the Library. | So was I. | I wasn't. |
| I like pizza. | So do I. | I don't. |
| I watched TV all day long. | So did I. | I didn't. |
| I can drive. | So can I. | I can't. |
| I'm not going to study. | Neither am I. | I am. |
| I wasn't at the hospital. | Neither was I. | I was. |
| I don't like the beach. | Neither do I. | I do. |
| I didn't enjoy that movie. | Neither did I. | I did. |
| I can't ski. | Neither can I. | I can. |

## Pattern Practice 2a: Match the agreements or disagreements to the correct statements.

1. _____ I can't swim very well.
2. _____ I got up late this morning.
3. _____ He doesn't like to exercise.
4. _____ I didn't go anywhere yesterday.
5. _____ I like to go snowboarding.
6. _____ He was at school.

a) Neither do I.
b) Oh, I don't.
c) So did I.
d) So was I.
e) Neither can I.
f) I did.

## Pattern Practice 2b: Now fill in the blanks to complete the conversations.

1. A) I want to go to France on my next vacation.
   B) ______________________________. That sounds very romantic.
2. A) I didn't like that movie.
   B) ______________________________. I thought it was very entertaining.
3. A) I drink eight cans of soda a day.
   B) ______________________________. It is too sweet for me.
4. A) I don't like going to the library.
   B) ______________________________. I like studying at home.
5. A) I can't play sports very well.
   B) ______________________________. But I'm good at playing video games.
6. A) I'm going to see a movie tonight.
   B) ______________________________. I have tickets for the eight o'clock show.

## Pattern Practice 2c: Circle the correct reply to each statement.

**1.** A) I went to church last weekend.

B) So did I. / Neither did I.

**2.** A) We didn't go to school yesterday.

B) So did I. / Neither did I.

**3.** A) I don't like hamburgers.

B) So did I. / I love them.

**4.** A) I don't have enough time to study.

B) Neither do I. / I hate them.

**5.** A) I can't stand the cold weather.

B) Neither did I. / Neither can I.

**6.** A) We were in a car accident this morning.

B) So was we. / We weren't.

**7.** A) Tim is allergic to water.

B) Neither was he. / So is Ted.

**8.** A) Mike likes whole wheat bread.

B) His wife hates it. / So doesn't his wife.

**9.** A) Jack hates fighting.

B) So does his sister. / Neither do I.

**10.** A) I think it's too hot in here.

B) So did I. / So do I.

## Dialogue (Listening and Speaking):

Listen to the dialogue and fill in the missing words. Then practice the dialogue with your partner twice.

| |
|---|
| **Emily:** Hi Rob, are you excited about Halloween? |
| **Rob:** Yeah, Halloween is awesome! I love it. |
| **Emily:** (1) _______________! I love dressing up and getting candy. |
| **Rob:** Cool! I always wear a fun **costume**. Last year, I was a zombie. |
| **Emily:** (2) _______________! I was a zombie and **scared** my brother. |
| **Rob:** That's funny! Do you like scary movies? |
| **Emily:** (3) _________________. they're too **scary** for me. |
| **Rob:** Really? I love scary movies! They're so cool. That's why I went to a **haunted house** last year. |
| **Emily:** (4) ___________________. I'm scared to go. |
| **Rob:** Haunted houses are fun! They're scary but **thrilling**. |
| **Emily:** Yes, maybe I'll try to go to a haunted house this year. |
| **Rob:** You should try it. I am excited for Halloween this year! |
| **Emily:** (5) __________________! |

**Key words:** costume 복장 / scared 무섭게 했다 / scary 무서운 / haunted house 유령의 집 / thrilling 흥미진진한

**Reading:** Read the following story and then answer the questions.

### Tom's Birthday Party

My name is Tom, and I want to tell you about my birthday party last weekend.

I invited all my friends to my house to celebrate. Everything was going well until my friend Mike started **complaining.**

"There's too much cake." he said. "I don't like cake."

"But I do." I said. "I love cake, **especially** chocolate cake."

"Maybe we need to go somewhere else." Mike said. "I like playing video games."

"So do I." I agreed. "Let's clean up and go to the **arcade**. We can listen to music **on the way** there."

"I love rock music!" Mike said.

I just wanted Mike to be happy, so we drove to the arcade and listened to his favorite music.

**Key words :** complaining 불평하는 / especially 특히 / arcade 오락실 / on the way 가는 도중에

## Reading Questions:

1. Who is telling the story?

______________________________

2. Does Mike like cake?

______________________________

3. Does Tom like cake?

______________________________

4. Does Tom like playing video games?

______________________________

5. Where did Tom and Mike go after the party?

______________________________

## Conversation Practice: Ask and answer the questions with a partner.

1. What are some ethnic foods you've tried? How were they?
2. What is your favorite movie genre? What's your favorite movie title?
3. What are some extreme sports you would like to try?
4. What are your favorite holidays? What do you do on those days?
5. Do you have any souvenirs? What are they?

## Editing: Find and correct the errors in the following sentences.



1. A: I'm going to the beach.

   B: So do I. I'm going with my friends after lunch.

2. A: I studied for the test.

   B: Neither do I. I don't think I will get a good score.

3. A: I love watching horror movies.

   B: So can I. Horror movies are thrilling.

4. A: I wasn't at the party.

   B: So was I. I was at home studying.

5. A: I can't play the guitar.

   B: So can I. I learned how to play 2 years ago.

Unit 12

# Review

## Unit 07: Does she like jazz or pop?

**Vocabulary:** Match the music genres with the correct Korean definitions.

| | |
|---|---|
| **1.** pop | a. 재즈 |
| **2.** hip-hop | b. 록 음악 |
| **3.** classical | c. 리듬 앤 블루스 |
| **4.** jazz | d. 팝 음악 |
| **5.** R&B | e. 레게 음악 |
| **6.** electronic | f. 일렉트로닉 |
| **7.** rock | g. 발라드 |
| **8.** Latin | h. 컨트리 음악 |
| **9.** reggae | i. 힙합 |
| **10.** ballad | j. 고전 음악 |
| **11.** country | k. 라틴 음악 |

## Practice 1: Fill in the blanks using ***or***, ***but***, or ***and***.

1. My favorite Italian foods are pasta ___________ pizza.
2. Should we take the subway ___________ a taxi?
3. She can sing ___________ dance very well.
4. The movie was too long ___________ interesting.
5. Do you want to go to the zoo ___________ the museum?
6. We can go to the restaurant now ___________ later.
7. Concerts are fun, ___________ there are too many people.
8. In the mornings, I wake up ___________ brush my teeth.

## Practice 2: Fill in the blanks using ***because*** or ***so***.

1. He turned off the lights ___________ he was going to bed.
2. He woke up late, ___________ he was late for school.
3. They went to the beach ___________ it was a sunny day.
4. He wore sunglasses ___________ the sun was too bright.
5. She bought a new phone, ___________ she could video call with her friends.
6. They went to the park ___________ they wanted to enjoy the nice weather.
7. The cake was delicious, ___________ they ate another slice.
8. She brought her camera ___________ she could take photos of the sunset.

**Reading:** Read the following story and then answer the questions.

**Taylor Swift**

Taylor Swift is a famous singer from America. She sings and writes songs that many people like. Some of her most popular songs are “Love Story”, “Shake It Off”, and “Blank Space”.

People enjoy her music because it’s fun and easy to listen to. Taylor writes about her life, so her songs feel real.

Taylor performs in many concerts around the world, **including** in countries like the United States, Canada, and the United Kingdom. Thousands of fans go to her concerts to see her sing. Fans all over the world love her music and **admire** her talent.

**Key Words:** including 포함하여 / admire 존경하다, 감탄하다

## Reading Questions:

1. What is one reason people enjoy Taylor Swift’s music?

   a. It’s difficult to listen to
   b. It’s fun and easy to listen to
   c. It’s sad and emotional
   d. It’s loud and noisy

2. Which countries does Taylor Swift perform her concerts?

   a. Only in the United States
   b. Only in Canada
   c. Only in the United Kingdom
   d. In many countries around the world

3. How do fans feel about Taylor Swift’s music?

   a. They love it and admire her talent.
   b. They find it boring.
   c. They don’t like it.
   d. They don’t care about it.

## Unit 08: What would you like to order?

**Vocabulary:** Match the dishes with the correct pictures.

1. _____ Spaghetti
2. _____ Pad Thai
3. _____ Caesar Salad
4. _____ Turkey Sandwich
5. _____ Pizza
6. _____ Pho
7. _____ Risotto
8. _____ Vegan Panini

a. 
b. 
c. 
d. 
e. 
f. 
g. 
h. 

**Practice 1:** Fill in the blanks using ***would***, ***could*** or ***may***.

1. Server: What ____________________ you like?
2. Child: ____________________ you pass me the pepper?
3. Worker: ____________________ I help you?
4. Coworker: I ____________________ like to visit Spain someday.
5. Student: ____________________ I ask you a question?
6. Friend: ____________________ you read this?
7. Professor: Where ____________________you like to go?

**Practice 2:** Rewrite the sentences in the correct order.

1. you / like to / how / pay / would

   ______________________________________________?

2. carry / could / you / my luggage

   ______________________________________________?

3. leave / I / may / the room

   ______________________________________________?

4. you / would / what / like

   ______________________________________________?

5. to New York / book / would / I / like to / a flight

   ______________________________________________.

**Dialogue:** Listen to the dialogue and answer the questions.

| |
|---|
| **Server:** Welcome to Sunny Cafe! How may I help you today? |
| **Customer:** May I take a look at the menu, please? |
| **Server:** Certainly, here you go. |
| **Customer:** Thank you. What would you recommend? |
| **Server:** Our special today is tuna sandwich and our caesar salad is popular. |
| **Customer:** That sounds delicious. I'd like tuna sandwich and caesar salad, please. |
| **Server:** Excellent choice! May I offer you any drinks with that? |
| **Customer:** Yes, I would like a glass of iced tea, please. |
| **Server:** Of course! And would you like any dessert? |
| **Customer:** What kind of desserts do you have? |
| **Server:** We have cheese cake, apple fie, and chocolate lava cake. |

| | |
|---|---|
| **Customer:** I'll have a slice of chocolate lava cake, please. |
| **Server:** Wonderful! Will that be for here or to go? |
| **Customer:** For here, please. |
| **Server:** Your order will be ready shortly. Enjoy your meal! |



## Dialogue Questions:

1. What did the customer order for their main dish?

   a. chicken club sandwich c. tuna sandwich

   b. veggie sandwich d. steak and cheese sandwich

2. What drink did the customer want?

   a. lemonade c. soda

   b. iced tea d. water

3. What dessert did the customer choose?

   a. cheese cake c. apple pie

   b. chocolate brownies d. chocolate lava cake

# Unit 09: What should I do?

**Vocabulary 1: Body:** Write the English words for the Korean meanings.

1. 어깨 ______________________
2. 무릎 ______________________
3. 골반 ______________________
4. 허리 ______________________
5. 이마 ______________________
6. 허벅지 ______________________
7. 팔꿈치 ______________________
8. 종아리 ______________________
9. 엄지손가락 ______________________
10. 턱 ______________________

**Vocabulary 2: Health Problems:** Write the English words for the Korean meanings.

1. 감기 ______________________
2. 두통 ______________________
3. 복통 ______________________
4. 치통 ______________________
5. 불면증 ______________________
6. 인후염 ______________________
7. 열 ______________________
8. 비듬 ______________________

**Practice 1:** Match the following health problems with suggestions.

| | | |
|---|---|---|
| 1. ______ insomnia | | a. drink some warm milk |
| 2. ______ broken finger | | b. take some vitamin C |
| 3. ______ no energy | | c. go see a doctor |
| 4. ______ have a cold | | d. take medicine |
| 5. ______ small cut on the finger | | e. put on some ointment |

**Practice 2:** Fill in the blanks with the correct health problems.

1. A: I have ________________________. What should I do?
   B: You should see a dentist.
2. A: I have ________________________. What should I do?
   B: You should use special shampoo.
3. A: I have ________________________. What should I do?
   B: You shouldn't drink coffee or use your cell phone before bed time.
4. A: I have ________________________. What should I do?
   B: You should take some medicine and put a hot pack on your stomach.
5. A: I have ________________________. What should I do?
   B: You shouldn't speak too much or smoke cigarettes.

**Dialogue:** Listen to the dialogue and answer the questions.

| |
|---|
| **Seth:** Hey, I have a stomachache and it doesn't go away. |
| **Anna:** Oh no, that's not good. Maybe you should try to drink some **ginger** tea. |
| **Seth:** I tried, but it didn't help. |
| **Anna:** Hmm, did you eat anything spicy? Sometimes spicy food can **upset** your stomach. |
| **Seth:** Yeah, I had some spicy noodles for lunch. |
| **Anna:** Well, maybe you should **avoid** spicy food for a while. Did you also have a **heavy meal**? |
| **Seth:** Yeah, I had a big dinner last night. |
| **Anna:** Maybe you should try to eat lighter meals for a few days. Also, you shouldn't forget to drink enough water. |
| **Seth:** You're right. I'll try that. Thanks, Anna. |
| **Anna:** No problem, Seth. If you're not feeling better tomorrow, you should see a doctor. |

**Key Words:** ginger 생강 / upset 불편한 / avoid 피하다 / heavy meal 무거운 식사

## Dialogue Questions:

1. What health problem does Seth have?

   a. stomachache  c. backache

   b. headache  d. sore throat

2. What suggestion does Anna give to Seth to help him his headache?

   a. eating spicy food  c. drinking ginger tea

   b. avoiding caffeine  d. taking a break from screens

3. What does Anna tell Seth to do if he doesn't feel better tomorrow?

   a. take a nap  c. drink more coffee

   b. see a doctor  d. go for a walk

## Unit 10: What do you have to do?

**Vocabulary:** Write the English words for the Korean meanings.

1. 허용된: ____________
2. 금지된: ____________
3. 합법적인: ____________
4. 불법적인: ____________
5. 엄격한: ____________
6. 관대한: ____________
7. 통금 시간: ____________
8. 최고의: ____________
9. 최저의: ____________
10. 연령 제한: ____________

**Practice:**

Fill in the blanks using ***should***, ***shouldn't***, ***has/have to***, or ***don't have to***.

1. I ____________ be at work at 9am tomorrow.
2. The students ____________ play cellphone games in class.
3. She ____________ take a test to enter university.
4. You ____________ eat less rice if you want to diet.
5. You are too skinny. You ____________ gain some weight.
6. Students ____________ do P.E. in Shingu College.
7. You ____________ get some rest. You look very tired.
8. High school students ____________ wear uniforms in Korea.
9. We ____________ drink alcohol before running in the marathon.
10. You ____________ buy a ticket to watch a movie at CGV.

## Reading:

Choose "***should***", "***has/have to***", "***shouldn't***" or "***don't have to***".

**Korea Army**

In Korea, almost every young man (1) ________________________ join the **army.** Women (2) ________________________ go to the army. If men go too late, they will (3) ________________________ take **orders** from younger guys. In Korea, it can be **uncomfortable** to give orders to an older person or take orders from a younger one. Their hair (4) ________________________ be less than 3cm long, so they (5) ________________________ get a haircut before joining. In the first month, they (6) ________________________ do **physical training.** So, they (7) ________________________ do some basic exercises before they go. Once they're in the army, they (8) ________________________ wake up at 6 AM and go to bed at 10 PM.

**Key Words:** army 군대, 육군 / orders 명령 / uncomfortable 불편한 / physical training 신체 훈련

## Unit 11: Do you like spicy food?

**Vocabulary:** Match the Korean meanings with the English phrases.

| | | |
|---|---|---|
| 1. ______ bland | | a. 호러 |
| 2. ______ comedy | | b. 코미디 |
| 3. ______ ethnic food | | c. 로맨스 |
| 4. ______ food poisoning | | d. 멋진 경치(전망) |
| 5. ______ horror | | e. 기념품 |
| 6. ______ martial arts | | f. 무술 |
| 7. ______ romance | | g. 민족 음식 |
| 8. ______ scenic view | | h. 식중독 |
| 9. ______ spicy | | i. 매운 |
| 10. ______ souvenir | | j. 싱거운 |

**Practice 1:** Agree (동의하다) with the following sentences.

1. A: I'm hungry. B: ______________________________.
2. A: I was late. B: ______________________________.
3. A: I play games. B: ______________________________.
4. A: I ate pizza for lunch. B: ______________________________.
5. A: I can sing well. B: ______________________________.
6. A: I'm not happy. B: ______________________________.
7. A: I wasn't bored. B: ______________________________.
8. A: I don't like fish. B: ______________________________.
9. A: I didn't drink coffee. B: ______________________________.
10. A: I can't ride a bicycle. B: ______________________________.

**Practice 2:** Disagree (동의하지 않다) with the following sentences.

1. A: I'm hungry. B: ________________________________.
2. A: I was late. B: ________________________________.
3. A: I play games. B: ________________________________.
4. A: I ate pizza for lunch. B: ________________________________.
5. A: I can sing well. B: ________________________________.
6. A: I'm not happy. B: ________________________________.
7. A: I wasn't bored. B: ________________________________.
8. A: I don't like fish. B: ________________________________.
9. A: I didn't drink coffee. B: ________________________________.
10. A: I can't ride a bicycle. B: ________________________________.

**Dialogue:** Listen to the dialogue and answer the questions.

| | |
|---|---|
| Noah: | Hey, did you hear Taylor Swift's new pop song? |
| Olivia: | Yeah, I listened to it. I like it a lot! |
| Noah: | So do I! Taylor Swift makes great pop music. |
| Olivia: | **Definitely**! Her songs are perfect for dancing. |
| Noah: | I love pop music, but I'm not a fan of Michael Jackson. |
| Olivia: | Neither am I. His pop songs are good, but I don't like his R&B songs. |
| Noah: | Neither do I, but I am a fan of R&B. |
| Olivia: | **Totally**! What songs do you like? |
| Noah: | I **prefer** songs from Brown Eyes. Let's listen to some songs together! |
| Olivia: | Sure! I'll **give it a try**. |

**Key Words:** definitely 확실히 / totally 완전히 / prefer 선호하다 / give it a try 시도해보다

## Dialogue Questions:

1. What does Olivia think about Taylor Swift's new pop song?
   a. She dislikes it.
   b. She hasn't listened to it.
   c. She likes it a lot.
   d. She prefers R&B music.
2. How does Noah feel about Michael Jackson's music?
   a. He loves both his pop and R&B songs.
   b. He dislikes both his pop and R&B songs.
   c. He likes his pop songs but not his R&B songs.
   d. He likes his R&B songs but not his pop songs.
3. What does Olivia say to Noah about R&B music?
   a. She agrees with him.
   b. She disagrees with him.
   c. She listens to it every day.
   d. She suggests they listen to pop music.

# Answer Key

## Unit 01

### Pattern Practice 1a:

1. niece
2. uncle
3. brother
4. grandfather
5. father
6. niece
7. nephew
8. mother
9. cousin
10. grandmother

### Pattern Practice 1b:

1. cousin
2. aunt
3. nephew
4. sister – in – law
5. cousin

### Pattern Practice 2:

1. a. Who's that?
   b. That's my aunt.
   a. What's her name?
   b. Her name is Irene.
2. a. Who's that?
   b. That's my brother.
   a. What's his name?
   b. His name is Jessie.
3. a. Who's that?
   b. That's my sister – in – law.
   a. What's her name?
   b. Her name is Robin.
4. a. Who's that?
   b. That's my nephew.
   a. What's his name?
   b. His name is Eric.

**5.** a. Who's that?

b. That's my son.

a. What's his name?

b. His name is John.

## Pattern Practice 3:

**1.** a. Who owns that bicycle?

b. That's my sister's bicycle. It's hers.

a. Oh really? I didn't know that was your sister's bicycle.

**2.** a. Who owns that jacket?

b. That's Jenny's brother's jacket. It's his.

a. Oh really? I didn't know that was Jenny's brother's jacket.

**3.** a. Who owns that juice?

b. That's my cousin's juice. It's his/hers.

a. Oh really? I didn't know that was your cousin's juice.

**4.** a. Who owns that house?

b. That's Dale's parents' house. It's theirs.

a. Oh really? I didn't know that was Dale's parents' house.

**5.** a. Who owns that dog?

b. That's my niece's dog. It's hers.

a. Oh really? I didn't know that was your niece's dog.

## Dialogue:

**1.** niece **2.** nephew **3.** his

**4.** yours **5.** our

## Reading Questions:

1. Jane invited her **mom**, **dad**, **brother**, **sister-in-law**, and **cousins**.
2. The **son's** toys were on the floor.
3. He borrowed his sister's **Barbie doll**.
4. He felt **embarrassed**.
5. She put it in **her room**.

## Editing:

1. Stacy picked up **her** doll and put it in **her sister's** hands.
2. I bought a new laptop. This laptop is **mine**.
3. The Koreans flew **their** country's flag on Independence Day.
4. **My** cousin is coming to **my** house to visit.
5. What's **your** phone number? Can I save it in **my** phone?

# Unit 02

## Vocabulary 1a:

| | | | | |
|---|---|---|---|---|
| **1.** g | **2.** c | **3.** h | **4.** b | **5.** f |
| **6.** a | **7.** d | **8.** e | **9.** i | **10.** j |

## Vocabulary 1b:

| | | | | |
|---|---|---|---|---|
| **1.** e | **2.** a | **3.** h | **4.** c | **5.** f |
| **6.** b | **7.** d | **8.** g | **9.** j | **10.** i |

## Pattern Practice 1:

**1.** There is **2.** There are **3.** There is

**4.** There are **5.** There is

## Pattern Practice 2:

1. There was
2. There were
3. There were
4. There was
5. There were

## Pattern Practice 3:

1. Are there
2. Was there
3. Are there
4. Were there
5. Is there

## Pattern Practice 4:

1. There is a whiteboard in the classroom.
   There aren't students in the class
2. There are two elevators.
   There aren't people. (There are no people.)
3. There is a laptop and a cellphone.
   There aren't books.

## Dialogue:

1. There were
2. there were
3. Were there
4. there were
5. There's

## Reading Questions:

1. It is in Singapore.
2. There are many shops and restaurants.
3. There are fast food restaurants, cafes, and even fancy restaurants.
4. Yes, there are.
5. Yes, there are gardens, places to relax, and take a nap.

## Editing:

1. There is a pen on the table.
2. There are many restaurants near school.
3. Are there any baseball teams in Korea?
4. There are students eating in the cafeteria.
5. There aren't many taxis in the morning.

# Unit 03

## Vocabulary 1:

### Appearance:

| | | | | |
|---|---|---|---|---|
| **1.** g | **2.** o | **3.** q | **4.** l | **5.** b |
| **6.** n | **7.** h | **8.** j | **9.** e | **10.** k |

### Character:

| | | | | |
|---|---|---|---|---|
| **1.** c | **2.** r | **3.** s | **4.** p | **5.** d |
| **6.** f | **7.** a | **8.** m | **9.** i | **10.** t |

### Word bank:

1. good – looking
2. attractive
3. ugly
4. neat
5. plain
6. honest
7. kind
8. strange
9. fun
10. selfish

## Vocabulary 2:

1. pony tail
2. eyebrows
3. bald
4. brunette
5. mustache
6. curly hair
7. eyelashes
8. straight hair
9. freckles
10. blonde
11. beard
12. wavy hair

## Pattern Practice 1:

1. adjective: elderly, noun: father
2. noun: basketball player, adjective: tall
3. noun: children, adjective: young
4. noun: man, adjective: muscular
5. noun: girl, adjectives: that/short
6. adjectives: these/two/black, noun: pens
7. adjective: lazy, noun: children
8. adjectives: diligent/chubby, nouns: chef/customer
9. adjective: cold, noun: pizza
10. adjectives: windy/fallen, nouns: weather/trees

## Pattern Practice 2:

1. is, has, is
2. is, has, has
3. has, is, is, is
4. is, has
5. has, is

## Dialogue:

1. short
2. slim
3. blonde
4. serious
5. smart
6. young
7. elderly

## Reading Questions:

1. Aunt Sarah
2. She has curly brunette hair and brown eyes.
3. Greg is humorous.
4. The youngest child has wavy brown hair.
5. Everyone in the family is diligent.

## Editing:

1. He is short and has black hair.
2. My father is chubby and is bald.
3. My best friend is petite and is patient.
4. Jennifer is attractive and slim, but she is stubborn.
5. The men have long beards and mustaches.

# Unit 04

## Vocabulary:

| | | | | |
|---|---|---|---|---|
| **1.** c | **2.** e | **3.** b | **4.** a | **5.** h |
| **6.** i | **7.** j | **8.** f | **9.** d | **10.** g |

## Pattern Practice 1:

1. cheaper than
2. smaller than
3. more intelligent than
4. warmer than
5. more important than
6. quieter than
7. younger than
8. more expensive than
9. slower than
10. more comfortable than

## Pattern Practice 2:

1. better than
2. farther than
3. noisier than
4. sunnier than
5. more than
6. less than
7. smellier than
8. messier than
9. worse than
10. lovelier than

## Pattern Practice 3:

1. older than
2. harder than
3. nicer than
4. more expensive than
5. better than
6. more difficult than
7. farther than
8. earlier than
9. more useful than
10. bigger than

## Dialogue:

1. smaller than
2. stronger than
3. easier than
4. bigger
5. compare

## Reading Questions:

1. The Internet is a big web. It connects people and information.
2. People used phones and letters to talk to each other.
3. They started in the 1960s.
4. The Internet got bigger.
5. Yes, it is.

## Editing:

1. Terry runs faster than Michael.
2. My friend is worse than me in singing.
3. This class is more interesting than my other classes.
4. The boys are taller than girls in the class.
5. Summer is hotter than winter.

# Unit 05

## Vocabulary 1:

| | | | | |
|---|---|---|---|---|
| **1.** f | **2.** d | **3.** h | **4.** g | **5.** a |
| **6.** c | **7.** b | **8.** e | **9.** i | **10.** j |

## Pattern Practice 1:

1. Younger than / the youngest
2. more intelligent than / the most intelligent
3. warmer than / the warmest
4. more important than / the most important
5. quieter than / the quietest
6. cheaper than / the cheapest
7. slower than / the slowest
8. more comfortable than / the most comfortable
9. more expensive than / the most expensive
10. smaller than / the smallest

## Pattern Practice 2:

1. messier than / the messiest
2. more than / the most
3. sunnier than / the sunniest

4. worse than / the worst
5. smellier than / the smelliest
6. better than / the best
7. farther than / the farthest
8. less than / the least
9. noisier than / the noisiest
10. lovelier than / the loveliest

## Vocabulary 2:

1. d  2. a  3. b  4. c  5. i
6. f  7. j  8. e  9. g  10. h

## Pattern Practice 3:

1. harder than / the hardest
2. cooler than / the coolest
3. hotter than / the hottest
4. more beautiful than / the most beautiful
5. more awful than / the most awful

## Dialogue:

1. people  2. the cheapest  3. the biggest
4. rental car  5. the most

## Reading Questions:

1. Japan is famous for colorful leaves in autumn.
2. Japan is the closest country for Koreans to visit.
3. The Great Wall is famous in China.
4. People travel to Shanghai to try new food in markets.
5. Thailand is the best option for many Koreans.

## Editing:

1. Lotte World Tower is the tallest building in South Korea.
2. Durian is the smelliest food.
3. Russia is bigger than Canada.
4. Samsung makes the best phones.
5. Seoul has the most people in South Korea.

# Unit 06

## Unit 01:

### Vocabulary:

| | | | | |
|---|---|---|---|---|
| 1. j | 2. h | 3. i | 4. d | 5. f |
| 6. a | 7. e | 8. c | 9. b | 10. g |

### Practice 1:

| | | |
|---|---|---|
| 1. your | 2. my | 3. his |
| 4. her | 5. her | 6. their |
| 7. our | 8. its | |

### Practice 2:

| | | | | |
|---|---|---|---|---|
| 1. yours | 2. his | 3. hers | 4. his | 5. mine |
| 6. hers | 7. mine | 8. yours | 9. theirs | 10. his |

## Unit 02:

### Vocabulary:

| | | |
|---|---|---|
| 1. coffee shop | 2. office | 3. bookstore |
| 4. cafeteria | 5. department office | 6. convenience store |
| 7. gym | 8. locker | |

## Practice 1:

1. There is 2. There is 3. There are
4. There was 5. There were 6. There were

## Practice 2:

1. Were there 2. Was there 3. Were there
4. Is there 5. Are there 6. Is there

## Dialogue Questions:

1. c 2. b 3. b

# Unit 03:

## Vocabulary 1:

1. d 2. j 3. h 4. g 5. a
6. i 7. b 8. f 9. c 10. e

## Vocabulary 2:

1. i 2. b 3. e 4. a 5. g
6. j 7. h 8. d 9. f 10. c

## Practice 1:

1. is, has 2. has, is 3. is, is, has 4. is, has, is

## Dialogue Questions:

1. a 2. d 3. b

## Unit 04:

### Vocabulary:

| | | | | |
|---|---|---|---|---|
| **1.** e | **2.** i | **3.** a | **4.** c | **5.** b |
| **6.** j | **7.** d | **8.** f | **9.** g | **10.** h |

### Practice:

**1.** hotter than
**2.** more expensive than
**3.** better than
**4.** sunnier than
**5.** more exciting than
**6.** farther than
**7.** friendlier than
**8.** worse than

### Reading Questions:

**1.** a **2.** c **3.** c

## Unit 05:

### Vocabulary:

| | | | | |
|---|---|---|---|---|
| **1.** e | **2.** l | **3.** h | **4.** b | **5.** a |
| **6.** k | **7.** c | **8.** i | **9.** f | **10.** d |
| **11.** g | **12.** j | | | |

### Practice:

| Adjective (형용사) | Comparative form (비교급) | Superlative form (최상급) |
|---|---|---|
| warm | warmer than | the warmest |
| bad | worse than | the worst |
| important | more important than | the most important |
| sunny | sunnier than | the sunniest |
| slow | slower than | the slowest |
| expensive | more expensive than | the most expensive |
| hot | hotter than | the hottest |
| far | farther than | the farthest |
| easy | easier than | the easiest |

## Reading Questions:

1. d  2. b  3. a

# Unit 07

## Pattern Practice 1:

| | | | | |
|---|---|---|---|---|
| 1. but | 2. and | 3. or | 4. and | 5. or |
| 6. but | 7. or | 8. and | 9. but | 10. or |

## Pattern Practice 2:

1. so
2. because
3. because
4. because
5. because
6. so
7. so
8. because
9. because
10. so

## Pattern Practice 3:

1. I went to the store, but I forgot to buy milk.
2. She loves to read books and watch movies
3. He studied all night, so he passed the exam.
4. We can go to the park, or we can visit the museum.
5. They wanted to watch a movie, but it was sold out.
6. I like to swim, so I joined the swim team.
7. She was hungry because I didn't eat breakfast.
8. We were tired, so we went to bed early.
9. He plays the guitar, and he sings.
10. Bring your jacket because it's cold outside.

## Dialogue:

**1.** or **2.** because **3.** but
**4.** so **5.** and

## Reading Questions:

1. No, BlackPink is a girl group.
2. It has four members: Jisoo, Jennie, Rose, and Lisa.
3. They sing a mix of pop, hip-hop, and dance.
4. Their songs often talk about love and confidence.
5. Yes, they talk to their fans on social media.

## Editing:

1. I like to listen to jazz music, **but** I don't like rock music.
2. I was late for school **because** I got up late.
3. He wanted to play soccer, **so** he called his friend to join him.
4. We can eat Chinese food **or** Italian food for lunch.
5. They can enjoy the concert **and** eat dinner together afterwards.

# Unit 08

## Pattern Practice 1a:

**2.** May / Could **3.** Would / Could
**4.** May / Could **5.** May

## Pattern Practice 1b:

1. Could you pass me the mustard?
2. Could you carry my suitcase?
3. What would you like to order?
4. I would like to have the cherry pie.
5. May I use the restroom?

## Pattern Practice 2:

1. I would like a glass of milk.
2. She would like to see the dessert menu.
3. My friend would like a slice of chocolate cake.
4. We would like some water.
5. He would like extra cheese on his pizza.

## Dialogue:

1. May
2. May
3. Could
4. would like
5. Would
6. Would

## Reading:

1. It means a restaurant that is famous for its delicious food.
2. People search online to visit these gourmet restaurants.
3. Some people wait in long lines to enter these hotspots.
4. They specialize in traditional Korean, Italian, Spanish, Vietnamese, and Thai dishes.
5. Customers post their photos on their social media platforms.

## Editing:

1. Would/Could you pass me the salt?
2. May I help you?
3. Would/Could you call me later?
4. Could you read this?
5. Would/Could you help my sister?

# Unit 09

## Vocabulary 1:

| | | |
|---|---|---|
| 1. head | 10. heel | 19. chest |
| 2. neck | 11. cheeks | 20. arm |
| 3. shoulder | 12. lips | 21. stomach |
| 4. back | 13. chin | 22. thumb |
| 5. elbow | 14. pelvis | 23. fingers |
| 6. waist | 15. leg | 24. thigh |
| 7. buttocks | 16. forehead | 25. knee |
| 8. calf | 17. eye | 26. foot |
| 9. ankle | 18. teeth | 27. hand |

## Vocabulary 2:

| | | |
|---|---|---|
| 1. dandruff | 2. insomnia | 3. a broken leg |
| 4. a toothache | 5. a headache | 6. a stomachache |
| 7. a fever | 8. a sore throat | 9. a cold |

## Pattern Practice 1:

1. has 2. have 3. have 4. have 5. has

## Pattern Practice 2:

1. a. Sam has a stomachache. What should he do?
   b. He should take some medicine, but he shouldn't eat spicy food.
2. a. I have insomnia. What should I do?
   b. You should drink warm milk, but you shouldn't drink coffee.
3. a. Sunny has a broken arm. What should she do?
   b. She should go to the emergency room, but she shouldn't exercise.
4. a. I have a toothache. What should I do?
   b. You should go to the dentist, but you shouldn't drink soda.

5. a. Kevin has a cold. What should he do?
   b. He should take vitamin C, but he shouldn't go outside without a jacket.

## Dialogue:

1. headache
2. should
3. shouldn't
4. should
5. shouldn't

## Reading Questions:

1. They went to a crowded amusement park.
2. They put their wallets in the back pockets.
3. She had a stomachache.
4. He had a headache.
5. They promised to always keep their wallets in a safe place.

## Editing:

1. She shouldn't eat too much candy.
2. You shouldn't drink coffee if you have insomnia.
3. She has a sore throat, so she should drink some tea.
4. You should go to the emergency room if you have a broken leg.
5. They have headaches and should rest.

# Unit 10

## Vocabulary 1:

1. d
2. g
3. f
4. j
5. c
6. b
7. a
8. e
9. i
10. h

## Pattern Practice 1:

1. should
2. don't have to
3. have to
4. shouldn't
5. have to
6. don't have to
7. shouldn't
8. have to
9. don't have to
10. have to

## Pattern Practice 2:

1. Jennifer has to study harder.
2. You have to wear safety glasses to work.
3. They should be more careful.
4. Bicyclists should wear helmets.
5. You have to be nineteen to vote.

## Dialogue:

1. curfew
2. should leave
3. have to follow
4. illegal
5. have to be

## Reading Questions:

1. Only the goalkeeper can touch the ball with hands.
2. The main point of soccer is to score goals.
3. Yes, they do.
4. No, they shouldn't.
5. Players have to use both hands to throw the ball.

## Editing:

1. I should stop smoking if I want to run the marathon.
2. Students shouldn't use their phones during class.
3. I don't like the sweater so I don't have to buy it.
4. Students shouldn't wear pajamas to school.
5. I'm only sixteen. I don't have to go to the army yet.

# Unit 11

## Word Bank:

**Ethnic foods:** sushi, taco, pasta, curry

**Extreme sports:** bungee jumping, sky diving, rock climbing, surfing

**Movie genres:** drama, comedy, action, horror, romance

**Holidays:** Christmas, New Year's Day, Thanksgiving, Halloween, Valentine's Day

## Pattern Practice 1:

**1.** I / it
**2.** I / stand
**3.** I / it
**4.** I / like
**5.** It's

## Pattern Practice 2a:

**1.** e
**2.** c
**3.** a
**4.** f
**5.** b
**6.** d

## Pattern Practice 2b:

**1.** So do I.
**2.** I did.
**3.** I don't.
**4.** Neither do I.
**5.** Neither can I.
**6.** So am I.

## Pattern Practice 2c:

**1.** So did I.
**2.** Neither did I.
**3.** I love them.
**4.** Neither do I.
**5.** Neither can I.
**6.** We weren't.
**7.** So is Ted.
**8.** His wife hates it.
**9.** So does his sister.
**10.** So do I.

## Dialogue:

**1.** So do I
**2.** So was I
**3.** I don't
**4.** I didn't
**5.** So am I

## Reading Questions:

1. Tom is telling the story.
2. No, he doesn't.
3. Yes, he does.
4. Yes, he does.
5. They went to the arcade.

## Editing:

| | | |
|---|---|---|
| 1. So am I. | 2. I didn't. | 3. So do I. |
| 4. Neither was I. | 5. I can. | |

# Unit 12

## Unit 07:

### Vocabulary:

| | | | | |
|---|---|---|---|---|
| 1. d | 2. i | 3. j | 4. a | 5. c |
| 6. f | 7. b | 8. k | 9. e | 10. g |
| 11. h | | | | |

### Practice 1:

| | | |
|---|---|---|
| 1. and | 2. or | 3. and |
| 4. but | 5. or | 6. or |
| 7. but | 8. and | |

### Practice 2:

| | | |
|---|---|---|
| 1. because | 2. so | 3. because |
| 4. because | 5. so | 6. because |
| 7. so | 8. so | |

## Reading Questions:

1. b　　2. d　　3. a

# Unit 08:

## Vocabulary:

| | | | |
|---|---|---|---|
| 1. g | 2. b | 3. c | 4. e |
| 5. d | 6. a | 7. f | 8. h |

## Practice 1:

| | | |
|---|---|---|
| 1. would | 2. Would/Could | 3. May |
| 4. would | 5. May | 6. Could |
| 7. would | | |

## Practice 2:

1. How would you like to pay?
2. Could you carry my luggage?
3. May I leave the room?
4. What would you like?
5. I would like to book a flight to New York.

## Dialogue Questions:

1. b　　2. b　　3. c

# Unit 09:

## Vocabulary 1:

| | |
|---|---|
| 1. shoulder | 6. thigh |
| 2. knee | 7. elbow |
| 3. pelvis | 8. calf |
| 4. waist | 9. thumb |
| 5. forehead | 10. chin |

## Vocabulary 2:

1. a cold
2. a headache
3. a stomachache
4. a toothache
5. insomnia
6. a sore throat
7. a fever
8. dandruff

## Practice 1:

1. a  2. c  3. b  4. d  5. e

## Practice 2:

1. a toothache  2. dandruff  3. insomnia
4. a stomachache  5. a sore throat

## Dialogue Questions:

1. a  2. c  3. b

# Unit 10:

## Vocabulary:

1. allowed
2. forbidden
3. legal
4. illegal
5. strict
6. lenient
7. curfew
8. maximum
9. minimum
10. age limit

## Practice:

1. have to
2. shouldn't
3. has to
4. should
5. should
6. don't have to
7. should
8. have to
9. shouldn't
10. have to

### Reading:

1. has to
2. don't have to
3. have to
4. has to
5. should
6. have to
7. should
8. have to

## Unit 11:

### Vocabulary:

1. j
2. b
3. g
4. h
5. a
6. f
7. c
8. d
9. i
10. e

### Practice 1:

1. So am I.
2. So was I.
3. So do I.
4. So did I.
5. So can I.
6. Neither am I.
7. Neither was I.
8. Neither do I.
9. Neither did I.
10. Neither can I.

### Practice 2:

1. I'm not.
2. I wasn't.
3. I don't.
4. I didn't.
5. I can't.
6. I am.
7. I was.
8. I do.
9. I did.
10. I can.

### Dialogue Questions:

1. c
2. c
3. a

# Workbook

## Unit 01: Who is your uncle?

### Vocabulary 1:

1. 딸: ____________________
2. 아들: ____________________
3. 부모님: ____________________
4. 자녀: ____________________
5. 외동: ____________________
6. 이모, 고모: ____________________
7. 삼촌: ____________________
8. 사촌: ____________________
9. 조카(여): ____________________
10. 조카(남): ____________________
11. 할아버지: ____________________
12. 친척: ____________________

### Vocabulary 2:

her, his, its, my, our, their, your

1. 나의: ____________________
2. 당신의/당신들의: ____________________
3. 그의: ____________________
4. 그녀의: ____________________
5. 그것의: ____________________
6. 우리의: ____________________
7. 그들의: ____________________

### Practice 1:

1. Who is your mother's father? ____________________
2. Who is your aunt's daughter? ____________________
3. Who is your sister's husband? ____________________
4. Who is your brother's son? ____________________

5. Who is your cousin's father? ______________________

6. Who is your sister's daughter? ______________________

7. Who is your wife's father? ______________________

8. Who is your father's sister? ______________________

**Practice 2:** Fill in the blanks with a possessive form or possessive pronoun.

1. Helen made ______________ bed in the morning. **(she)**
2. The keys are on the table. I think they're ______________. **(you)**
3. Freddy showed me ______________ photos of his trip to Europe. **(he)**
4. Sam lost his phone, but Amanda found ______________. **(she)**
5. Do you want to take your car or ______________? (I)
6. Did you bring ______________ umbrella? **(you)**
7. These are the students' textbooks. They are ______________. **(they)**
8. Whose dog is this? I think it's ______________. **(he)**

## Unit 02: Is there a coffee shop?

### Vocabulary:

| | |
|---|---|
| 1. 편의점: ______________ | 6. 체육관: ______________ |
| 2. 놀이공원: ______________ | 7. 미술관: ______________ |
| 3. 서점: ______________ | 8. 사무실: ______________ |
| 4. 식당: ______________ | 9. 커피숍: ______________ |
| 5. 사물함: ______________ | 10. 학과 사무실: ______________ |

**Practice 1:** Fill in the blanks using ***is*** or ***are***.

1. There ___________ a pen on the table.
2. There ___________ many students in the classroom.
3. There ___________ a new café in town.
4. There ___________ some computers in the office.
5. There ___________ a party tomorrow night.

**Practice 2:** Fill in the blanks using ***was*** or ***were***.

1. There ___________ a lot of people at the concert last night.
2. ___________ there any cookies left in the kitchen?
3. There ___________ a problem with the computer yesterday.
4. ___________ there any messages for me?
5. There ___________ a nice t-shirt at the department store, but now it's gone.

Practice 3: Fill in the blanks using ***is***, ***are***, ***was***, or ***were***.

1. ___________ there a movie theater near your house when you were a child?
2. There ___________ some delicious cakes at his house last night.
3. ___________ there a restroom nearby?
4. There ___________ a lot of people at the beach last summer.
5. ___________ there any good movies playing at the cinema?
6. ___________ there any interesting places in your hometown now?
7. There ___________ a lot of people outside around 6PM.

8. __________ there any problems with the Internet yesterday?

9. There __________ a popular restaurant in the city.

10. __________ there any difficult classes this semester?



## Unit 03: What's he like?

### Vocabulary:

funny, lazy, elderly, stubborn, friendly,
muscular, reliable, diligent, chubby, patient

| | |
|---|---|
| 1. 연로한: ______________________ | 6. 믿을 수 있는: ____________________ |
| 2. 근면한: ______________________ | 7. 게으른: ______________________ |
| 3. 친절한: ______________________ | 8. 근육의: ______________________ |
| 4. 통통한: ______________________ | 9. 웃기는: ______________________ |
| 5. 참을성 있는: __________________ | 10. 완고한: _____________________ |

**Practice:** Choose ***is***, ***are***, ***has***, or ***have***.

1. Hugh Jackman ___________ a moustache and a beard.
2. He ______________ patient and friendly.
3. She _____________ medium length blonde hair.
4. He ______________ a big nose.
5. The boy _____________ dark spiky hair.
6. The little girl _______________ stubborn.
7. The old man _________________ bald.

8. Pippy ______________ medium length red hair and small ears.

9. My best friend ________________ reliable.

10. Thor ____________ blonde hair and blue eyes.

11. Hulk ______________ muscular and diligent.

12. Koreans ____________ dark brown hair and dark brown eyes.

13. Parents ____________ patient with their children.

14. Men in the army __________________ short hair.

15. People from Busan ________________ fun and honest.

16. The comedian ________________ chubby.

17. Children don't ________________ moustaches.

18. It is difficult to be a flight attendant if you _____________ short.

19. You shouldn't play at the meeting. It _______________ serious.

20. The students ____________ shy. They don't raise their hands.

## Unit 04: Which is bigger?

### Vocabulary:

app, charger, file, laptop, notification,
printer, search engine, settings, website, wireless

| | |
|---|---|
| 1. 프린터: ____________________ | 6. 웹사이트: ____________________ |
| 2. 파일: ____________________ | 7. 무선: ____________________ |
| 3. 설정: ____________________ | 8. 노트북: ____________________ |
| 4. 검색 엔진: ____________________ | 9. 알림: ____________________ |
| 5. 충전기: ____________________ | 10. 앱: ____________________ |

**Practice:** Fill in the blanks using **comparatives (비교급)**.

1. Sarah is ______________________ **(beautiful)** her sister.
2. This book is ______________________ **(interesting)** the one I read last week.
3. My dog is ______________________ **(friendly)** yours.
4. Today is ______________________ **(sunny)** yesterday.
5. The blue car is ______________________ **(expensive)** the red one.
6. She is ______________________ **(talented)** at playing the piano __________ her brother.
7. This movie is ______________________ **(exciting)** the one we saw last night.
8. John is ______________________ **(intelligent)** Justin.
9. Summer is ______________________ **(hot)** autumn.
10. The new smartphone is ______________________ **(advanced)** the old one.
11. This restaurant has ______________ **(good)** food __________ the one we went to last week.
12. The movie we watched last night was ______________________ **(bad)** we expected.
13. My house is ______________________ **(far)** your house.
14. I have ______________________ **(little)** homework __________ you.
15. Coke has ______________ **(many)** calories __________ Pepsi.

## Unit 05: What is the fastest?

### Vocabulary:

accommodation, arrival, baggage, carry-on luggage, departure, passenger, passport, reservation, sightseeing, souvenir

| | |
|---|---|
| 1. 기념품: ________ | 6. 여권: ________ |
| 2. 숙소: ________ | 7. 도착: ________ |
| 3. 관광: ________ | 8. 출발: ________ |
| 4. 휴대 수하물: ________ | 9. 예약: ________ |
| 5. 수하물, 짐: ________ | 10. 승객: ________ |

**Practice:** Fill in the blanks using **superlatives (최상급).**

1. February is ________ month of the year. **(short)**
2. Rock climbing is ________ sport. **(dangerous)**
3. Pigs are ________ animals. **(dirty)**
4. My grandfather is ________ person in my family. **(old)**
5. Dolphins are ________ animals in the sea. **(intelligent)**
6. Russia is ________ country in the world. **(large)**
7. BTS is ________ K-pop group. **(famous)**
8. Lotte World Tower is ________ building in South Korea. **(tall)**
9. Nineteen years of age is ________ one can get a driver's license. **(early)**
10. Gangnam is ________ place to live in South Korea. **(expensive)**

## Unit 07: Does she like jazz or pop?

### Vocabulary:

1. 록 음악: ____________________
2. 발라드: ____________________
3. 팝 음악: ____________________
4. 재즈: ____________________
5. 고전 음악: ____________________
6. 라틴 음악: ____________________
7. 레게 음악: ____________________
8. 힙합: ____________________
9. 일렉트로: ____________________
10. 리듬 앤 블루스: ____________________
11. 컨트리 음악: ____________________

**Practice:** Choose the correct answer to complete the sentence.

1. I was late for class this morning ________ the bus was late.

   a) so b) because c) but

2. I usually go home at four o'clock, ________ then I watch TV for an hour.

   a) and b) because c) or

3. My classmate studies very hard, ________ she always gets good grades.

   a) because b) but c) so

4. Would you like tea ________ coffee?

   a) so b) but c) or

5. Thomas was really hungry this morning ________ he didn't eat breakfast.

   a) but b) so c) because

6. We went to the airport, ________ we forgot to bring our suitcases.

   a) but b) so c) or

7. Cathy decided to order spaghetti, ________ Gary decided to order a pizza.

   a) so b) and c) because

**8.** I was very sick yesterday, ________ I didn't go to work.

a) because b) so c) but

**9.** You can do the homework now ________ later.

a) or b) but c) because

**10.** I spilled my drink ________ I wasn't careful.

a) because b) so c) and

**11.** My bedroom was very cold ________ I forgot to close the window.

a) because b) so c) or

**12.** I can either take Korean Air ________ Asiana from Incheon to LA.

a) or b) but c) and

**13.** First we drove to the airport, ________ then we got on the plane.

a) but b) or c) and

**14.** It's raining outside, ________ you should take your umbrella.

a) but b) or c) so

**15.** I don't feel very well, ________ I think I'll go to see a doctor.

a) but b) so c) because

**16.** Sarah called her friend, ________ nobody answered the phone.

a) so b) because c) but

**17.** I saw my teacher this morning, ________ I asked him about the test.

a) and b) but c) or

**18.** Did we win ________ lose the soccer match with Germany?

a) but b) or c) and

**19.** They felt very bored, ________ they turned on the TV and watched a movie.

a) but b) so c) because

## Unit 08: What would you like to order?

### Vocabulary:

1. 올리브: ______________________
2. 상추: ______________________
3. 양파: ______________________
4. 겨자: ______________________
5. 오이: ______________________
6. 치즈: ______________________
7. 얇게 썬 달걀: ______________________
8. 토마토: ______________________
9. 소금: ______________________
10. 후추: ______________________

**Practice 1:** Write from most polite to casual using ***Can***, ***May***, ***Could***, or ***Would***.

Polite 공손한: ______________________ I…?

______________________ I…?

Casual 일상적인: ______________________ I…?

Polite 공손한: ______________________ you…?

______________________ you…?

Casual 일상적인: ______________________ you…?

**Practice 2:** Rewrite the sentences to polite form using "***would like***".

1. I want a Caesar Salad.

______________________________________________

2. They want four cups of Cappuccino.

______________________________________________

3. She wants some frozen yogurt.

_______________________________________________

4. He wants a burger and fries.

_______________________________________________

5. My friends and I want to eat spaghetti.

_______________________________________________

## Unit 09: What should I do?

### Vocabulary:

1. 무릎: ____________________
2. 허벅지: ____________________
3. 골반: ____________________
4. 어깨: ____________________
5. 이마: ____________________
6. 발목: ____________________
7. 엄지손가락: ____________________
8. 볼: ____________________
9. 발뒤꿈치: ____________________
10. 가슴: ____________________
11. 허리: ____________________
12. 팔꿈치: ____________________
13. 종아리: ____________________
14. 엉덩이: ____________________

**Practice:** Choose ***has***, ***have***, ***should***, or ***shouldn't***.

1. Cara ______________ insomnia.
2. Sandy ______________ big feet.
3. Do you ______________ a stomachache?
4. I ______________ dandruff again.
5. Teddy ______________ a headache.

6. He ________________ a runny nose.

7. She ________________ a cough.

8. Do you ________________ any allergies?

9. I ________________ a sore throat.

10. Stella ________________ a fever.

11. I ________________ a broken arm. I ________________ see a doctor.

12. Mom ________________ a stiff neck. I ________________ give her a massage.

13. Did she ________________ a stomachache? She ________________ eat a lot.

14. My brother ________________ a toothache. He ________________ eat sweets.

15. I ________________ dirty hands. I ________________ touch important paperwork.

## Unit 10: What do you have to do?

### Vocabulary:

age limit, allowed, curfew, forbidden, illegal,
legal, lenient, maximum, minimum, strict

1. 최고의: ________________
2. 최저의: ________________
3. 불법적인: ________________
4. 합법적인: ________________
5. 엄격한: ________________
6. 관대한: ________________
7. 통금 시간: ________________
8. 연령 제한: ________________
9. 허용된: ________________
10. 금지된: ________________

**Practice:** Choose ***should***, ***shouldn't***, ***have to***, or ***don't have to***.

1. You ______________________________ eat less rice if you want to diet.
2. You ______________________________ buy a ticket if you want to watch a movie at CGV.
3. The students ______________________________ play cell phone games in class.
4. You ______________________________ study Spanish at Shingu College.
5. The drink is free, you ______________________________ pay for it.
6. You ______________________________ smoke cigarettes on the subway.
7. If you want to travel abroad, you ______________________________ bring your passport.
8. Did you break your leg? You ______________________________ go to the hospital.
9. When you go inside a building, you ______________________________ wear a mask.
10. Boys ______________________________ use the girls' bathroom.

## Unit 11: Do you like spicy food?

### Vocabulary:

bland, comedy, ethnic food, food poisoning, horror, martial arts, romance, scenic view, spicy, souvenir

| | |
|---|---|
| 1. 매운: ______________________ | 6. 민족 음식: ______________________ |
| 2. 싱거운: ______________________ | 7. 식중독: ______________________ |

3. 기념품: ____________________

4. 경치: ____________________

5. 로맨스: ____________________

8. 코미디: ____________________

9. 무술: ____________________

10. 호러: ____________________



**Practice:** Agree (동의하다) and disagree (동의하지 않다) with the statements.

1. I can drive well.

   Agree: ____________________

   Disagree: ____________________

2. I sing very well.

   Agree: ____________________

   Disagree: ____________________

3. I'm not sleepy.

   Agree: ____________________

   Disagree: ____________________

4. I watched the new movie last night.

   Agree: ____________________

   Disagree: ____________________

5. I'm going to the library after school.

   Agree: ____________________

   Disagree: ____________________

# Campus English 102

**Authors:** Charles Kim (Shingu College)
Jieun Hwang (Shingu College)
Yoondo Bae (Shingu College)

**Publisher:** Shingu Publishing Co.

**Design:** eundesign

**ISBN:** 978-89-7668-285-7 03740

February 2025 Printing


Published by Shingu Publishing Co.
377, Gwangmyeong-ro, Jungwon-gu, Seongnam-si
Gyeonggi-do, South Korea
Tel. 031-741-3055